To John Cain,

with the best wishes

of

Oliver Stutchbury

25.1.44.

TOO MUCH GOVERNMENT?

A Political Aeneid

By the same author

THE USE OF PRINCIPLE

TOO MUCH GOVERNMENT?

A Political Aeneid

OLIVER STUTCHBURY

THE BOYDELL PRESS

Published by The Boydell Press,
PO Box 24, Ipswich IP1 1JJ

ISBN 0 85115 081 0

Made and printed in Great Britain by
The Garden City Press Limited
Letchworth, Hertfordshire SG6 1JS

CONTENTS

CHAPTER ONE

A CONSERVATIVE START

I WAS born on 22 January 1927, the youngest of the four sons of my marvellous mother, who also brought into the family the house in which I now live and am writing this account of my life-long attempt to succeed in politics. My father was a consulting mining engineer and City of London businessman who died when I was eleven. I went to a public school (Radley), served as an officer in the Grenadier Guards just after the 1939–45 war, and then went up to King's College, Cambridge. With such a background, it is hardly surprising that on coming down to earn my living in the City, I should (in 1950) choose to pursue my political ambitions in the Conservative cause.

I had another reason for joining the Conservative Party. My first cousin (and godfather) Gareth Maufe, who had been a powerful influence on my life after my father's early death, was then the treasurer of the Chelsea Conservative Association. I asked Gareth whether he would get me a humble job licking on stamps or something of that order. He worked quickly, and shortly afterwards I found myself assistant secretary of the Chelsea Conservative Association's Political Education Committee. An exceedingly active body it was too, filled with the spirit of the "two-way movement of ideas" (i.e. from Central Office to the constituencies, and vice versa). It was at that time producing a report on "The Worker in Industry". Meetings were held in the members' houses. Minutes were read and approved. Drafts were prepared, studied and revised. Resolutions were passed, although I doubt whether very many of us (office workers to a man) would have recognised a worker in industry if he had seen one. All the same, as I now perceive, that committee was manned by some exceptionally competent people for a body which was so far removed from the levers of real political power.

I was sometimes impatient of my colleagues' contributions. I noticed, and tried to correct, a character defect which has dogged me all my life. To make things more entertaining, I like to put forward ideas in a way which will stimulate interest. But this sometimes shocks people, and people do not like being shocked. I also talked too much. "If you want to get on, keep your mouth shut, dear boy", counselled Gareth. Sometimes I took his advice. "A very successful meeting of the Political Education Committee in the evening," I wrote in my diary, "in which I succeeded in being so silent that it was remarked upon on all sides. There was even some talk of allowing me to speak."

I made friends with the Conservative Party's agent in Chelsea and early in 1951 I told him that in the event of a dissolution of Parliament I would take a month off from my office and, paying my own expenses, would help the Conservatives wherever they most needed help. He put me in touch with J. V. Garmonsway, the Area Agent for Wales, who was the first person in politics to give me a leg-up. When I met Garmonsway, he surprised and delighted me by asking if I would like to stand as a candidate. Gareth had warned me that I must expect to be treated as the lowest of the low until I had worked my passage, and such an exciting possibility had not entered my head. I explained to Garmonsway that I had taken no steps to have myself put down on the list of approved candidates; but he said that this omission did not matter. He might be left with a vacant constituency at the last moment in which case he would try and insinuate me. In case this didn't happen, he sent me down to spend a beery week-end at Barry—a marginal constituency in which he said he would want me to work if I did not get a constituency of my very own.

When the dissolution of Parliament was announced in the autumn of 1951 I rang up Garmonsway and continued at intervals to be a nuisance to him. I was staying with my mother at an hotel in Droitwich, where she was taking the baths to ease the rheumatic troubles which beset her at that trying period in her life. On Tuesday, 25 September we were trying to wrestle with our home farm accounts when there was a knock on the door and a waiter said I was wanted on the telephone. It was someone called Frazer calling from Port Talbot, the Aberavon constituency—a division of Glamorgan. There was to be an executive meeting on Thursday at which they might adopt me as their candidate.

It was raining when I set off on Thursday, and although I could (and did) dream of the brilliant parliamentary career which was opening up before me, I couldn't help feeling that the start was inauspicious. Near Merthyr I nearly had a nasty accident when a girl riding a bicycle suddenly swerved in front of me. I knocked her off the saddle but I was luckily going very slowly and she was not hurt. I helped her on again and drove on through Ebbw Vale and Tredegar and was appalled by the black squalor of what I saw. I had never before been exposed to the industrial areas of South Wales. When I got down to Port Talbot, things did not look quite as bad as they had in the valleys.

My adversary in the selection contest was a charming Major McLaren who was staying at the same hotel as I was. At 7.30 that evening Frazer arrived with the vice-chairman of the local association, and we all piled into a very old car and went to the local committee rooms. There was gathered there a motley assortment of housewives, crusty old professional men and the rising lights of the Young Conservatives. I judged them to be, on the whole, a very fair cross-section of the constituency's Tories. We were led through the assembly to an office at the back of the hall and left alone to muster our courage together. I batted first and was asked to tell the committee "my views". I fancied that I really put myself over rather well. Although I hadn't much experience of Welsh problems myself, I told them, my father had been a mining engineer in the principality and he had told me a lot about it. So I had a little knowledge of the work many of the electorate were engaged in; we were facing a critical election; and so on. Then it was McLaren's turn, and then we waited an interminable time.

At 9.30 the vice-chairman came in and broke the news that it had been decided to let McLaren's name go forward, but softened the blow to my pride by saying that there were several people present who were very disappointed that I hadn't been allowed to go on. I thus missed the chance of opposing the Labour incumbent, who was Walter Padley. It was probably just as well because when, years later, I was to be found working at Transport House, he was one of the members of the N.E.C. whom I used to try to lobby into improving the Labour Party's organisation, and an earlier encounter on opposing sides at a general election would have been no help to my cause. In the event, McLaren did not fight Aberavon but was destined for a distinguished career as Member for Bristol, North-west.

I left the hotel at 9.30 the next morning and drove to Cardiff where I saw Garmonsway. It was my youth they had objected to, he said. He seemed delighted that I had come along and mentioned that there was still a chance of a constituency to fight. He introduced me to his assistant, a Miss James, and on Wednesday, 3 October, Miss James rang me up to say that I was going to fight Rhondda East. There would be no time for any selection procedure, I would just be adopted as the Conservative candidate. "What fun!" I said, though afterwards I wondered if it was an altogether appropriate reaction.

Rhondda East (Harry Pollitt's old constituency), I was to discover, was a one-industry coal-mining constituency, compactly situated in a Welsh valley. In the mining villages, clustered round the colliery, row upon row of small identical houses built in the nineteenth century were occasionally broken up by a pub or a shop or a club. The year before, in the 1950 general election, the Labour Party had had a majority of 22,182 over a Communist who had won 4,463 votes. The Conservative came in a bad third with 2,634 votes, tailed by the Welsh Nationalist with 1,357.

Polling day was on Thursday, 25 October, and I spent the next three weeks in "my constituency" getting an invaluable blooding in one of the drearier tasks of politics: although I understand that electioneering comes to be enjoyed by the career politician, which only goes to show how a person's natural inclinations can be distorted by the passage of time. My agent had been seconded to Wales from Central Wandsworth for the duration of the campaign. He seemed to me to be a bit of a defeatist by temperament, which perhaps explains why he had been allowed to leave Central Wandsworth (which was a marginal constituency) in their hour of need. But he had a nice wife who came and helped. As far as I could ascertain we three (and my eldest brother, Dombey, who came up with the farm van for part of the campaign) were the only Conservative workers in the valley. We set up our headquarters in the Wyndham Club in Porth.

I bought an Ordnance Survey map of the constituency, drew up a plan of how I would try to cover the whole constituency, and prepared to wage battle. The speech I made when I was unanimously adopted as Conservative candidate on Tuesday, 9 October was very fully reported in the *Porth Gazette and Rhondda Leader* on the following Saturday. According to that paper I gave a "penetrating analysis of the nation's present critical situation" and claimed that my party had the answer to the national problems. The speech does not read too badly today, and I stuck to it pretty closely during the rest the campaign. "Decline in value of money: my party's main argument" was the caption on a brief biography of the twenty-four-year-old standard-bearer of capitalism. The Conservatives were, I claimed, going to halt the rise in the cost of living by reducing Government expenditure and increasing industrial production. Pretty corny stuff, but dead on the party line.

The solid foundation (such as it was) of the Tory vote was said to centre on the membership of the Conservative Working Men's Clubs. This was a mistaken idea. In those days, the pubs in Wales were closed on the Sabbath. The Conservative Club members in my constituency were people who wanted a drink on Sundays but who had been excluded from the (more respectable) Labour Party Working Men's Clubs. Some of the Conservative Clubs, indeed, were dominated by members of the Communist Party. There was one particular club in Ferndale where I had the stormiest meeting of the campaign. Members were wearing the hammer and sickle in their lapels and one called me a snorting spiv. Not to be outdone, another said I should be snorting well shot for being a Conservative. I could scarcely make myself heard, and retired with a sore throat but exhilarated from having survived my first hostile meeting. (Never embark on an old-fashioned election campaign without many *different sorts* of throat lozenge to hand: one brand can be monotonous.)

In the mornings I would go canvassing in the villages. We fixed a loudspeaker to the top of Dombey's van and would drive to the map reference I had assigned to myself for that day. I would get out and address the empty street. "Voters of Pontygwaith. My name is Oliver Stutchbury and I am the Conservative candidate in this constituency. We are facing a critical election. . . . I am down here to put forward the Conservative case: and I am now going to walk down the street. If any of you would like to put any questions to me about Conservative policy or argue with me, I shall be very pleased to meet you irrespective of what political party you belong to." By the time I had finished this rigmarole, one or two doors would be open, and a few inquisitive faces would show from inside the houses. As I walked down the street (and I had walked the length of the built-up part of the constituency by the end of the campaign) most people would have retired indoors and closed the door. The ones who were left would smile in a friendly sort of way if I smiled first. Most of them would say: "We haven't got anything to conserve," and then laugh at their own joke. Or: "It's Labour, we are." Sometimes: "Churchill's a warmonger." In the evenings I had one and sometimes two meetings, usually in the village schools, where I was listened to with politeness and natural courtesy by an audience that ranged between two and fifty in number.

Churchill, I discovered to my great surprise, was a serious electoral liability in the valleys. What had happened or what had not happened in Tonypandy in 1910 was still a burning political issue. There was one Conservative voter who claimed to have been present on that never-to-be-forgiven occasion. He swore that the troops had *not* fired on the colliers. But nobody believed him. As it had been some seventeen years before I was born, I found the controversy puzzling and uninteresting.

On the other hand, Anthony Eden was deeply respected. He was a gentleman, I was told. Why did I not get him to come and speak for me at the cinema in Porth? I would get an overflow audience. Alas, I explained, he had more important things to do. The miners noted with many a sly dig that Conservative Central Office had (very sensibly) written off the valleys. No politician of any kind (or anyone else for that matter) spoke for me during the campaign.

On Friday, 19 October I lost my temper (for the first time during the campaign) with someone in Trealaw who said that I had £800 with which to fight the campaign. I called him a liar and he said he would stuff me down the drain at the side of the road. However, we did not come to blows, and when I met him later, at the count, he went out of his way to be my friend and introduce me to the Labour notables. I began to take note of the irrationality of individual decision-taking in politics. When the people of the Rhondda told me that they were going to vote Labour because Churchill was a warmonger, they were going to vote Labour but not for the reason they gave. Very many of them had spent the 1930s out of work and starving under a Tory Government. Intellectually, I argued, this was a bad reason for voting Labour in 1951; but emotionally it was the best of all possible reasons and I knew it. Indeed, I was obliged to concede that were I in their shoes I would do the same. The point was that the reason they gave was not the real reason. All they were doing by saying that Churchill was a warmonger was rationalising a decision which they had already taken in their bellies. I know that all this is very old stuff to political commentators. It was quite new to me, fresh from college with a degree in philosophy and still clinging to the simple hope that man was a rational animal.

On polling day, a Conservative supporter from outside the constituency dressed his Land-Rover up to look like a Christmas tree and I toured in it around all the polling booths. There were no Conservative tellers to chat up anywhere except in Penygraig, and all was not conducted exactly according to the book. Thus there were Labour tellers inside the schools making perfectly sure that each voter knew who the Labour candidate was, but (as everyone knew) it could not conceivably affect the outcome. For the Conservative candidate it was fun to be racing around. Whenever I saw a group of people I waved to them, and as often as not they waved back, for all that they were inclined to the view that all Tories should be hanged. To reach every polling booth took all day.

The count took place on Friday at the Kings Hall in Pentre after the count for Rhondda West was finished. Walking round the tables as the votes were being counted, it looked to me as if I had not achieved a single blessed vote. My friend from Trealaw introduced me to Mark Harcomb—the father of the Labour Party in the valleys. He tried to be rude, but seeing that this did not upset me we discussed other things than politics and he ended up by being quite affable. I began to feel terribly hungry. The results were not ready by three o'clock and we had had no lunch. My agent came to say that he thought there was no hope of saving the deposit and that we would be lucky to poll as many votes as the Communist. Then, as they began to count in packets of one hundred votes, it turned out that there were six packets more for me than for him. The Labour people were simply delighted. I was making history for them in beating the Communist into third place.

The final result was:

Mainwaring, W. H. (Lab.)	27,958
Stutchbury, O. P. (C.)	3,522
Cox, I. (Comm.)	2,948
Lab. maj	24,436

Mainwaring proposed a vote of thanks to the returning officer and his staff, which I seconded. Then, when the results had been read out to the public outside the hall, Mainwaring made a speech, and with an odious lack of generosity went back into the hall again without waiting for me to say my few words to the largest crowd I had ever faced. So I turned to follow him in when the Labour women in the crowd shouted for me to say something as was only proper. So I congratulated Mr Mainwaring (making a point of pronouncing the "ware" because he himself liked to be known as "Mannering", to the secret scorn of many of his own supporters) and commiserated with Mr Cox for being in the same boat as myself in losing his deposit. Cox came forward and said: "No, I am not in the same boat as the Tory candidate and never shall be. The most disturbing feature of the election is that the Tory candidate has got nearly a thousand more votes than he did last time." He could not have paid me a more acceptable compliment.

Dombey and I said our farewells, got into the van, grabbed a sandwich in Porth and drove off through the night to arrive home in the early hours of Saturday morning. There I had a much appreciated bath and a long, deep sleep.

CHAPTER TWO

A CAUSE

MY sojourn in the Rhondda in October 1951 was one of the cheapest holidays I have ever spent. Central Office paid my lost deposit and all the expenses I had incurred which I would allow them to pay, including even my hotel bill. The person with whom I lost my temper in Trealaw was probably nearer the truth than I was.

Taking an active part in the campaign was valuable to me in a number of other ways. It gave me, in the eyes of some Conservatives, a completely spurious reputation for "bravery". The two Rhondda constituencies and Bethnal Green were the only seats at that election in which the Conservative candidate lost his deposit, and to be one of the three who had battled against such overwhelming opposition was thought to be "brave", despite my testimony to the contrary. It was valuable, too, in that it began to break down my nervousness as a public speaker. If one makes a very similar speech night after night and sometimes twice a night, it is difficult not to get a bit bored with it towards the end of the campaign. Boredom counteracts nervousness.

I gained one or two significant insights into the conduct of public figures from this concentrated burst of public speaking. If one speaks frequently in public, I found, it is difficult *not* to feel oneself obliged "to say a few words". Then one feels deprived unless one *is* allowed to say a few words: and the infection has become the disease, which is one of the very worst things about political life. I continue to be staggered by nearly every single politician's indifference to the boredom his speeches generate. It was only by passing a motion overwhelmingly at a meeting of the Labour Group on the Greater London Council, to which I was co-opted in 1973, that in 1975 we were able to stop chairmen of committees from making *two* long speeches to Council when their items came up. Exhortation from the Leader's Co-ordinating Group (his Cabinet) had no effect in stemming the flow. Every speech at any Labour Conference I have attended (particularly speeches from the platform—Harold Wilson being the worst offender in my experience) are twice as long as they need be. In the second half the speaker loses a lot of the sympathy he may have won in the first half. I understand from those who attend Conservative and Liberal Party Conferences that in this respect they are no different. Conservative Party Conferences were certainly no different in my day. But verbal inflation in politics is nothing new when one recalls the contemporary accounts of Gladstone's Budget speeches in the nineteenth century.

This concentration on the spoken word is the explanation of another disagreeable phenomenon: the banality of much of what goes for political discussion. To the politician who is seriously afflicted by the speaking disease, his thoughts begin to take shape in publicly utterable sentences—and consequently have to be "safe". Speech and thought being closely connected, it is but the twinkling of an eye before the patient tends only to think safe things. Now, safe thoughts are rarely (if ever) worth communicating: so politicians get involved in a boring circle in which anything new and risky tends, as a matter of psychological mechanics, to get excluded. But this is to digress.

After the 1951 election campaign I polished up my public speaking technique by attending an excellent course at Central Office run by David Allnutt, who was a genius at teaching people to speak in public. He taught us how to order our thoughts to maximum advantage and the importance of enjoying (or pretending to enjoy) the speech we were making. I would make no claim to be an accomplished public speaker myself (may I, indeed, be preserved from his temptations) but the techniques David Allnutt taught me made me better than I was. I began to rustle up speaking engagements for myself in order to get known among the faithful. I spoke in Central Wandsworth (to which my agent in Rhondda had returned), in Maida Vale, in Horley and in Wallington; nearer my home in the country I spoke in Herstmonceux, in Seaford and in Haywards Heath.

In the spring of 1953 I found a theme which was to become an obsession with me, and in due course was an important factor in causing me to leave the Tory party. My commitment to the Conservative cause had always been one of upbringing and not of intellectual conviction. I now hit upon a policy to which I became intellectually committed. On 22 April 1953 I spoke to the Wimbledon Young Conservatives about R. A. Butler's second Budget, propounding my new-found conviction that surtax should be abolished and the rate of estate duty increased to produce a corresponding amount of revenue. "I met with stiff opposition to my views," I noted in my diary, "as I fancy I shall always meet from Conservatives. But I'm sure I'm right."

This basic belief in the corrupting influence of inherited wealth and the fruitfulness of created wealth; and the economic importance of choking off the former and fostering the letter by fiscal legislation was a cause to which I remained faithful so long as I was a party politician. I have written three pamphlets and many articles on the subject; and made so many speeches, both public and private, as to be a bore to my family and friends. I do not repent. I think our economy would be far healthier today, and Britain would be a better place to live in, if the powers that be had thought the way I thought in the early 1950s and had acted accordingly over the years. It may seem to be a comparatively trivial issue. I do not regard it as such. One of the few matters upon which the nation state has complete autonomy is how it chooses to tax its citizens. There is thus no valid "force of circumstances" excuse if a country's taxation arrangements turn out to produce undesirable consequences.

The Young Conservatives of Norbury gave my proposals a better reception on 7 May. So did the Islington Y.C.s on 18 May and the North St Pancras Y.C.s on 28 May. I mention all these meetings not, alas, to be able to point to a groundswell of popular support for my cause (because, of course, my speeches were of no consequence whatever) but to point to evidence that I was not letting the grass grow under my feet. I was performing the tricks required of an aspiring politician with as much diligence as the most zealous could reasonably demand.

The most exciting event at that time in my political life was when, at the instigation of Humphry Berkeley (later the M.P. for Lancaster and author of *Crossing the Floor* (Allen and Unwin, 1972)), I became a member of the Coningsby Club. This insti-aution (which seems still to flourish, if its notices in *The Times* are tnything to go by) was composed of Conservative Oxbridge graduates who dined regularly in the Palace of Westminster and were addressed by a distinguished politician. Afterwards we were allowed to air our own views. Its members became all too conversant with my views on the corrupting influence of inherited wealth. Peter Tapsell (now the M.P. for Horncastle) tells me that on one occasion when Butler was the guest of honour and I had unburdened myself of my obsession, Butler privately begged leave to doubt if I were really a Conservative.

Meanwhile, I had taken steps to get myself on the list of approved Conservative candidates—noting wryly that the vice-chairman of the party in charge of candidates had been all over me with pleasure when he discovered that I did not want to have a stab at Bournemouth East (a safe Conservative seat which had just fallen vacant). Then, as an approved candidate, I began attending solemn candidate's conferences. There was one I particularly remember which was held at Church House, Westminster, on 29 March 1952. By chance, at lunch I sat next to a likeable scoundrel called Kirby, who later became Member of Parliament for Arundel and Shoreham. At that time he was a journalist working for a syndicate of American papers. A knowledge of Russian enabled him to cover the Iron Curtain countries in a way which, I am sure, would have suited the mood of the more militant of the extreme right in the States. He confided in me that all he was interested in was death. To my look of astonishment, he explained that he was interested in the death of Members of Parliament elected for reasonably safe Conservative seats. He had an infallible method, he went on, of winning Tory selection committees. Central Office would send down their own choice and he would arrive in his Rolls-Royce, wearing his Old Etonian tie, so he *made* enemies. Then there would be the local candidate and he would be bound to *have* enemies. And finally there would be Kirby. He would arrive in his little pre-war Morris Minor and would tell them, however large the majority, that he intended to fight the next election as if the constituency were a marginal seat. They loved that. He would say that he was going to turn the word TORY into VICTORY and give a loud cheer. Then he would get the nomination.

Some years later, depressed by repeated failures to get myself adopted as a Tory candidate anywhere, and impressed by Kirby's success, I myself tried the Kirby gambit at a Conservative selection committee. "I am going to turn the word TORY," I said bravely, "into VICTory." The horrible phrase froze in my mouth and I stumbled over the last four letters. Helen, my then newly-wedded wife who was sitting by my side, could scarcely believe her ears. The gimmick did not even succeed. But this, I am ashamed to own, was only one of a number of occasions in which I was not true to myself in my unsuccessful quest for a Tory seat.

I did not contest the 1955 general election and in retrospect this was a mistake. I could have fought Rhondda East again, had I wanted to. But there were two factors which weighed heavily in the scale against spending yet another holiday in the Welsh valleys. First, Helen was in the most disagreeable stage of her first pregnancy. I do not suppose that this would have been a sufficiently strong reason for someone as ambitious as I was then had it not been for an intriguing gamble. The sitting member of Parliament for a safe Conservative seat close to my family home was seriously ill of some unidentified disease and would be unable to campaign. I was on good terms with his agent. If I agreed to do the stricken member's meetings for him and made a success of them, I should stand quite a chance of succeeding him if death or permanent ill-health should take its beneficent toll. I did some of the sick man's meetings for him, but others had the same plan. We were all dished because he recovered, was re-elected and has lived happily ever afterwards. So that little ploy did not work. Moreover, having forced two of my brothers who lived in the constituency to join the local Conservative Association, I have had my leg pulled mercilessly about this episode ever since.

People who scoff at the poor quality of our politicians seem to have no inkling of how difficult it is to get into career politics. I wholly reject the argument which is sometimes put forward as an excuse for our present plight, that politics does not attract able people. Some of my very ablest contemporaries in both political parties have been dogged by persistent failure in getting selected and must, by now, be minded to throw in their hands. The converse is, alas, also true: some of the least able have been surprisingly successful in getting seats. There does not seem to be much rhyme or reason in it.

After the 1955 general election, I started to try in earnest to get myself adopted for a constituency. I was turned down at Uxbridge (17 January 1956), East Willesden (7 February 1956) and Barons Court (18 July 1956). That was the way of the world, but more depressing was my inability even to get *seen* at all by seats which were moderately safe. What on earth did one do? I asked myself. It was no use bewailing my lack of family connections in politics, which are such a conspicuous advantage to anyone lucky enough to possess them. Other people with no connections seemed to make progress, so the fault must lie in myself.

It is in this context that I would like to explain my bizarre conduct in volunteering to be recalled to the army at the time of the Suez episode. When I was demobilised in 1948, I had opted to join the Regular Army Reserves of Officers, because all that this would involve was reporting, in writing, once a year to the War Office. Of the other options available, the more enthusiastic soldiers among my contemporaries joined their local territorials, or the "Z" Reserves. They would have to do some training at least once a year and this I decided, in 1948, was far too much like hard work for someone who planned a future life as far removed from the army as possible.

I watched with some detachment the storm over the Suez canal blowing up in 1956. I thought, not for the last time quite mistakenly, that it was incredible that we should actually intervene with force. But when the Prime Minister announced that he was going to call up the Reserves, I thought (in a flash of inspiration) I saw an opening for myself. It was possible that if the British had a short sharp campaign in the Middle East in which they were successful (as seemed likely, the Egyptians being what they then were), that thereafter the Prime Minister might call a general election. Then, no class of person would be more likely to be popular with local Conservative selection committees than officers of smart regiments returning from a victorious campaign. I even looked further ahead and considered the possibility of this conflagration leading to the third world war. In that case I might as well be in the thick of it with the professionals at the very beginning. I would acquire seniority that way. Accordingly, I attended at Regimental headquarters in Birdcage Walk and told them that although, for business reasons, it was not an application I could make officially, I would like the lieutenant-colonel to know that I would be quite happy to be recalled, if wanted.

It was a move I had to keep entirely to myself. I had only just become a full partner in the firm of solicitors I had joined on coming down from Cambridge, and my other partners could scarcely be asked to approve my voluntarily absenting myself from the practice on a wild goose chase like this. I did not even dare to tell my wife for fear that the truth leaked out. I dared explain my behaviour only to an old Cambridge friend, Alastair Boyd (now Lord Kilmarnock), so that if anything went wrong and the truth about my volunteering came out, he would be in a position to establish my motives for a course of action which was, to say the least, a long shot.

We were spending the August Bank Holiday week-end in the country when a telegram arrived one sultry evening: "WAR OFFICE INTEND TO RECALL YOU FOR DUTY WITH 3RD BATTALION REPORTING WINDSOR 8 AUGUST—REGIMENTAL ADJUTANT". As I had kept my intrigue entirely secret from my family, there was no one with whom I could share my elation. Moreover, I was entirely unprepared for the effect this telegram had on Helen. Had I foreseen that she would be quite so upset, I doubt if I should have been ruthless enough to go ahead with my scheme. But by then there was no way out. The bottom seemed to fall out of her world for the moment, and now knowing the truth I don't think she has ever quite forgiven me. My mother, driving with me to the station, said in a resigned sort of way that it was the third occasion she had said goodbye to her men-folk going off to a war, and she only hoped that it was the last. It seems funny now that we should have so magnified the incident. But it didn't seem so funny then.

The received view is that the Suez expedition was inefficiently run from a military point of view. That was not my impression. It was not the fault of the military that the nearest harbour from which we could launch an invasion of Egypt was Southampton, which happened to be three weeks' sea-voyage away. Less than a week after rejoining the 3rd Battalion Grenadier Guards at Windsor, I was on the high seas bound for Malta. As far as I could judge, every episode of the expedition from beginning to end was carried out by the soldiers (not politicians) with a very high degree of efficiency. But that is another story. In my political Aeneid, I got back from foreign service just in time to face a committee selecting a Conservative candidate to oppose John Stonehouse at the Wednesbury by-election caused by Stanley Evans's resignation from Parliament because he supported Eden on Suez. They chose Peter Tapsell rather than me. It was probably just as well from my point of view because my partners could not have been expected to relish any further voluntary absenteeism from my place of work. I arrived home just in time for Christmas.

My Suez exploit seemed to improve my rating as an approved candidate, and I got asked to selection committees for better seats. In February 1957, an old Cambridge acquaintance, Marcus Kimball, who was by then well established as Conservative Member of Parliament for Gainsborough, was looking for an amenable colleague to fill a vacancy in a neighbouring constituency: Rutland and Stamford. He took one look at the *curriculum vitae* I was in the habit of sending to Conservative Associations looking for candidates, and made me change it altogether. Things I was proud of, like winning scholarships to Radley and Kings, he excised. In their place went things I had paid for, like membership of the Country Landowners' Association and the National Farmers Union. I had mentioned "playing the piano" as a hobby. "I am a bit doubtful about 'playing the piano'," wrote Marcus, "but perhaps that is only my own intolerance." I took it out and put "riding" instead.

It seemed to work. I reached the short list for South-East Leicester, but failed at the last fence. Despite Marcus's efforts I failed to get Rutland and Stamford. Brighton (Kemp Town), which would have suited us ideally, interviewed Helen and me, but chose David James. In September we failed once again at North Hammersmith. Setting it out like this in cold print, one would surmise that after as many failures I would have become insulated against the anguish of failing. Not so. Each failure at a selection committee and each letter of regret was an equally bitter blow to my pride and a source of fierce disappointment that I did not seem able to get started on the career I wanted more than any other.

My last attempt to secure a Conservative candidature—and the occasion on which I was nearest to success—was at Torrington in June and July 1958. The seat had been lost to a Liberal (Mark Bonham-Carter) in a by-election, but there was a very good chance of winning it back at a general election. Helen and I visited the constituency at their invitation on no fewer than three occasions to be interviewed by various committees, and there was correspondence with the chairman. On one occasion we came back to England from a holiday in Ireland especially to be present. I thought (and still think) that the chairman of the Constituency Association was doing all he could to further my candidature. I made what I thought was the speech of my life at the final selection meeting. But it didn't win me the candidature. In the end, they decided to choose none of us, and began the process of selection again from scratch. The chairman, apologising to me, explained that I was too like Anthony Royle—the unsuccessful candidate against Bonham-Carter who had decided to better his prospects by trying somewhere else and had thereby offended the Torrington Conservatives.

Another reason, I suspect, was that I took no pains to conceal my unpopular crusade on the subject of the taxation of the individual. The successful career politician cannot afford to have ideas of his own to which he is attached. He may become too attached to them and be unable to shed them when it becomes expedient to do so. If he is wise, he becomes a broker of other people's causes which he can discard when his customers won't buy, without losing face or his own self-respect.

CHAPTER THREE

CHANGING HORSES

SOME of my less than generous Conservative friends aver that I left their party because I failed to get a winnable seat. There is a grain of truth in this, but I would prefer to put it rather differently. As I have recounted, I never failed in my speeches to Conservative selection committees to mention that my particular hobby-horse was tax reform and one of the reforms I favoured was an increase in tax on inherited wealth to enable direct taxes on income to be reduced. This would have been very off-putting to Conservative audiences, because (as I now realise) a belief in the sanctity of personal property and in an individual's right to pass his land and possessions to whom he pleases, is at the very core of Conservative philosophy. My counter-argument that it was necessary to prune the old wood of inherited wealth to enable the young wood to grow and so let capitalism flourish, carried much less weight. Capitalism is not nearly so important a strand in Conservative philosophy as many people suppose. So I would prefer it to be thought that I left the party because I could foresee that, holding the views which I did and was not prepared to dissemble, I never would get a winnable Conservative seat. This is a rather different way of putting it than saying that I left because I failed to get a winnable seat.

In 1957 I had written my first pamphlet on tax reform and throughout 1958 I was trying to get it published. In it I argued that, owing to the vagaries of the British system of taxing the individual, it was more important to "make" money than to "earn" money (a distinction I owed to Clifford Barclay, a very, wise friend—a chartered accountant by training, he was the force behind the Oxford University Business School). Earning money, owing to confiscatory rates of tax in the higher income brackets, had become self-defeating; making money, which came about largely through gifts of one sort or another and was therefore untaxed at that time, was consequently much more important. This, I argued, was to get matters exactly the wrong way round. It could be remedied by three simple measures:

(1) the replacement of estate duty (a voluntary tax) by a progressive gifts tax (which in those days I dubbed a "Fortuitous Enrichment Tax") with the aim of preventing anyone from inheriting or being given property in excess of £20,000;

(2) the disallowance, in calculating income subject to tax, of any "expenses" incurred by a person or business which could be used by individuals in their ordinary living (e.g. entertaining, travelling, etc.); and

(3) the abolition of surtax to enable people in the higher brackets to pay these necessary expenses out of their taxed income.

On the advice of a friend, I sent my manuscript first to Staples Press Limited, who rejected it by letter dated 29 January 1958. The Insitute of Economic Affairs (Oliver Smedley) rejected it in a letter dated 17 March 1958. I sent it to the Conservative Political Centre and it was returned to me with a letter from Peter Goldman dated 2 October 1958 which I still treasure. "My dear Stutchbury," he wrote, "I am now returning your manuscript on tax reform. I found it enjoyable, stimulating, amusing, maddening, wrong-headed and a very hot potato. I am afraid the C.P.C. cannot publish it. There is all the difference in the world between flying unorthodox kites and indulging in eccentricities! But I hope you will be able to find someone a little less strait-laced than I to give it an airing." My friend Anthony Sumption, who was chairman of the Conservative Political Centre, was in hospital at the time suffering from a detached retina. He subsequently told me that had he been in action, he might well have got the decision reversed. In which case it is possible that I might never have left the Conservative Party. Who can tell?

At the end of 1958 my business career took an abrupt change of course. One of my firm's clients, whose work I was responsible for looking after, was the biggest group of unit trust managers in the City, then called Bank Insurance Trust Corporation Limited. Its manager was due to retire in a year or so and the directors were looking outside the company for his successor. I could see the immense possibilities in the business. The only snag to the job was that the board did not want as manager someone whose main preoccupation was politics. If I wanted the job I had to give an undertaking not to be a candidate for political office while I was doing it, so that I could devote all my energies to running the business.

I never had any real doubts about whether or not to accept the job on these terms. I was getting nowhere in politics and this job offered a challenge I could not resist. I moved to Bank Insurance as assistant manager on 1 January 1959. At the same time I resigned from the panel of approved candidates (and from the Coningsby Club), severed all my connections with the Conservative Party, and for the next six years devoted my best efforts to promoting the business of what in time, at my instigation, became known as the "Save and Prosper Group" of unit trusts. The unit trust industry was undergoing a transformation which had been sparked off by Edward du Cann when he launched his Unicorn Trust. The years 1959 to 1962 were years of unprecedented growth. When my predecessor retired I was appointed manager, and by 1961 I was managing director.

Meanwhile there remained the puzzling problem of how to get my (as I thought uniquely valuable) views on tax reform aired. As the Conservative Party would not publish them, I decided to try the Labour Party and sent the document to Percy Clark at Transport House. He sent it on to the Fabian Society and after some correspondence, W. T. Rodgers (the then secretary of the Fabians) wrote on 20 April 1959 that he thought he could now say that the Fabians would like to publish my draft. This was the moment in time when I first contemplated changing horses. In practice the Fabian Society did not publish my work for another ten years, but the seeds of my attachment to the Labour Party were sown when Bill Rodgers agreed in principle to publish my views. What happened in practice was that the draft went on to Jack Diamond (the then treasurer of the Fabians) who, accompanied by an assistant, gave me an excellent luncheon at the House of Commons on 23 June 1959 and asked for extensive alterations to be made in my text.

By now I was fed up with the whole thing and decided to publish it at my own expense. Hepburn and Sons Limited printed the work and it was published on 9 November 1959: with the forbidding title *A Tract on the Reform of Tax affecting the Individual*. With the help of Save and Prosper's public relations officer I was able to secure a certain amount of mention in the press. It was generously reviewed by the *Manchester Guardian* and the *Birmingham Post*. A short review appeared in the *Glasgow Herald*, and the *Economist* noticed it on 13 February 1960. I also sent a number of copies to Bill Rodgers, who distributed them (as I was later to discover) to some influential Labour Members of Parliament. But less than one hundred copies were sold and the arguments I advanced seemed to make no impression on anyone. I began to learn what I believed to be an important truth, that it really does not matter how right an idea may be: its rightness is not an important ingredient in its adoption. To get something done, I surmised, one needed to be in a position where one could press the necessary buttons. Even achieving such a position was not infallible, for one might only secure the position of power on the understanding that there were certain buttons which were not to be pressed. But one could face that hurdle when one came to it, the important thing was to get into the position of power.

When one reads biographies and autobiographies of politicians, one learns that, throughout their lives, they have tended to have a circle of friends who felt very much as they did on a range of political issues, and would meet occasionally to exchange views. All I can say is that this was not so for me. Until I met Winston Fletcher at about this time, there was no person of my acquaintance whose political attitudes seemed to coincide with mine in any significant way. Winston Fletcher was an advertising executive, who had read the moral science tripos at Cambridge as I had. He has since started his own agency and written a very funny book called *The Ad Makers* (Michael Joseph, 1973). I agreed with the Conservatives about the importance of capitalism but had for some time assented intellectually to Stephen King-Hall's argument in favour of nuclear disarmament. In July 1959, freed from my political party shackles, I began to contribute to the Campaign for Nuclear Disarmament. This was not exactly the action of someone on the right.

At the same time I couldn't swallow the Labour Party dogma of the importance of nationalising the means of production, distribution and exchange. I remember telling Bill Rodgers at a luncheon we had together at the City Club on 11 August 1959, when he persuaded me to become a member of the Fabian Society in order to receive its pamphlets regularly, that I did not think I would ever be able to become a member of the Labour Party because I found its dogma so unpalatable. He muttered something sympathetic. For the record, I would like to make it clear that I never even considered joining the Liberal Party, which seemed to me then (and I haven't changed my views since) to be a quaint historical anachronism. During the 1959 general election I was strictly neutral.

For a whole year I marked time politically—a member of no party and for that reason slightly uneasy. One of the disagreeable facts about British politics in my political lifetime has been that unless someone belongs to a major political party, he has no political future. It is all very well for Samuel Brittan to write books with provocative titles like *Left or Right The Bogus Dilemma*, (Secker and Warburg, 1968) and to propose new categories in place of Labour and Conservative which correspond more closely to the new differences in approach to contemporary problems. It is a nice idea but the fact remains that if someone has aspired to do anything in politics he has had to make the demeaning decision, which party should it be? When in my Labour days I was asked how I could ever have been a Tory, I was in the same position as I am in now, when I ask myself how I could ever conceivably have been Labour. An aspiring politician has no option but to tie the nearest appropriate political label to himself, keep quiet about his party's policies which he finds detestable, and continue his journey as best he may.

Let no one think that when I joined Save and Prosper I meant to spend the rest of my life in political purdah. I had renounced my political ambitions for a strictly limited period of time. After a full year as a political neuter, I felt the moment had come to test the water on the other side of the political divide. As I have mentioned, I was a supporter of the Campaign for Nuclear Disarmament. When the Labour Party at Scarborough in October 1960 "went unilateral" (a decision which Hugh Gaitskell said he would fight, fight, and fight again) I felt the time had come to join the fray on the unrespectable side of the fence.

Those who have not experienced it will not appreciate what a traumatic experience it is to join the Labour Party. With difficulty one discovers the address of the secretary of the Labour Party in whose constituency one votes and is directed to make inquiries of one's ward secretary (if any). The Barons Court Ward (in which Helen and I lived at the time) of the Barons Court Labour Party met monthly in a community centre just by West Kensington Underground Station. The utter purposelessness of its proceedings would have shaken off someone less determined than myself. The number at its meetings rarely exceeded ten. Of these, the hard core met regularly at the meetings of the Fulham Borough Council and the general committee of the C.L.P. They were the insiders and had private matters to discuss to which the outsiders (like myself) were not privy. For the rest, "administration" took most of the time. This was correspondence. Letters from the C.L.P. asking for resolutions, delegates, or money for good causes like regional or national conferences; help for other constituencies fighting by-elections; anything other than politics. I remember in particular one meeting which was wholly devoted to a debate on whether the ward typewriter (value approximately £2 10s.), should be insured with the Co-op as theretofore in accordance with good Socialist principles (at an annual premium of 18s. 6d.); or whether it should be insured by wicked private enterprise through a friend of one of the insiders (for 12s. 6d. annually). I was thought frivolous when I questioned whether it was worth insuring it at all. It was best to keep one's mouth shut in the Labour Party too.

They were friendly enough people except on an occasion when I let slip that although I was now a supporter of C.N.D., I had once been a Tory. Then a sort of animal pack hatred came to the fore. Just occasionally there was a political discussion, marked (when he was present) by some old-fashioned market-place oratory supplied by Bill Molloy who, to my intense surprise, became a Member of Parliament at the succeeding general election. But to pretend that the meetings had anything to do with politics would be to paint an entirely false picture. In my second year I was elected one of the ward auditors, but do not recall ever seeing any accounts. I dared not bring Helen along with me to ward meetings for fear she would find its proceedings incredible after her experiences in the Conservative Party, where there was lively political discussion, and laugh at me too much. She had not then any way, renounced her Conservative allegiance. The ward had been represented on the general committee of the constituency party by the same delegates for years and years. There was no chance of a newcomer achieving such an honour. Soon my business took me regularly to Scotland (where Save and Prosper owned a highly successful unit trust called "Scotbits") at the same time in the month as ward meetings and I became an irregular attender. But I was an avowed, if inactive, member of the Labour Party.

I began to write articles on quasi-political topics for the now defunct *Statist*. Paul Bareau, the editor, had been connected with my business for a number of years. He contributed an immensely popular readable newsletter which Save and Prosper distributed each month to bank managers, stockbrokers and other agents. Charming, urbane and well-informed, the monthly luncheons to which he came in order to discuss what he should write about that month, were one of the highlights of our routine in the office.

In early 1962 I became so incensed with the then received view (which his journal shared) that it was the duty of the monetary authorities to keep interest rates down, that I wrote him a long letter telling him how misguided this was. He replied that, although he disagreed with me, he would like to publish an article giving my argument because he thought that the people in the Bank of England should know that there was another point of view. I consulted my chairman as to whether this would constitute a breach of my undertaking not to indulge in politics, and (after consultations) he said that he thought I should contribute, if at all, under a pseudonym. I chose the name "Wycliffe" (described in the journal as "the chief executive of a City financial institution who wishes to remain anonymous") on the grounds that I could parry any direct question with the true reply that I had a twin brother of that name.

My first article—"The Case for Dear Money"—appeared in the issue of 23 March 1962. I still hold the views I put forward in that article. Am I right or am I being absurdly presumptuous in thinking that no one else in the U.K. was arguing at that time that dear money could be a good thing and should be encouraged? Milton Friedman was on this tack in America (as I later discovered), but I searched around Britain in vain, and when Norman Macrae published *Sunshades in October* (Allen and Unwin) in 1963, I distributed copies at my own expense to all my board.

Between March 1962 and April 1963 six articles by "Wycliffe" were published in the *Statist*. They included two rehashes of my tract: the "Case against Perquisites" and the "Case against Inherited Wealth" (which brought Paul Bareau a bagful of complaining mail and had to be replied to the following week by Timothy Raison); "Banks as Financial Supermarkets" (a policy I was then trying to further, to induce the clearing banks to sell more unit trust units—in those days they had no stake in my business); an article about the invalidity of the bankers' argument for non-disclosure of profits; and, finally, an argument in favour of a State Unit Trust (originally suggested by Nicholas

Davenport) to make National Savings honest. Making National Savings honest was another theme to which I was to return time and time again at intervals without any response.

Soon after this I wrote my most ambitious article thus far: "The Case for Unilateral Disarmament". It was a financial case. Britain just could not afford the expense of our defence budget—particularly its effect across the exchanges. I had argued out the financial C.N.D. case with the Prime Minister in Pratts one evening. Harold Macmillan had gently pointed out that it wasn't the nuclear arms but "the chaps" who cost the money. As a direct result of this encounter, I had become a unilateral disarmer, not just a unilateral nuclear disarmer. I have not changed my view on this despite the scorn of those who are quite rightly shrill on the evils and dangers of communism. I do not think we can any longer protect ourselves *by force* from these evils or dangers. Paul Bareau would not publish this article. I re-wrote it four or five times over the next two years and resubmitted it each time without success. So that was the end of "Wycliffe's" journalistic career and, for the time being, my exit from journalism. I had a lot of writing on my hands (I was producing the first draft of my *Management of Unit Trusts*) and persuaded myself that I had not the time or inclination to trouble myself with perverse editors. But I was frustrated and puzzled by Paul Bareau's refusal to publish one or other of these articles. I suppose I ought to have applauded his strength of mind.

One of the lessons I was to learn from this episode was that, if one wants a minority viewpoint expressed, one must get oneself into a position where no other man can frustrate the publication of one's views. This is an extraordinarily difficult position to attain unless one can speak from an institutional pulpit. No one since the war has managed it in politics except Enoch Powell. It is this difficulty which leads to people digging up Test Match pitches when they find that they cannot get their views aired in any other way. Although I cannot possibly approve this kind of behaviour, I have sympathy with people who do absurd things to get their grievances publicised.

CHAPTER FOUR

THE FIRST FRUSTRATING YEARS AT TRANSPORT HOUSE

IN a television interview at the time of the 1964 Budget, Jim Callaghan, who was Shadow Chancellor, expressed an interest in the idea of a State Unit Trust and, using this as an excuse for meeting him, I called on him to give him a copy of "Wycliffe's" article on the subject in the *Statist*. I also left him a copy of the article on the case against inherited wealth and tried to persuade him (without any success) that to legislate for a gifts tax in place of estate duty was the very first thing a Labour Chancellor should do when he got to No. 11 Downing Street. Jim was surprised to learn that I was a member of the Labour Party, and has been very kind to me ever since.

I worked very hard for Ivor Richard, our Labour candidate in Barons Court, at the time of the general election in the autumn of 1964. I deputised for Alan Clarke, the highly effective and pleasant party agent, when he was not in the office, I drove the candidate around when he wanted a chauffeur, I did my share of canvassing and rigged a loudspeaker on top of my car which relayed a charming message from the Barons Court Party's most distinguished member—Vanessa Redgrave—who explained why she would (in those far off days!) be voting Labour. Her message ended with her introducing her charlady who explained, in a rather different accent, why she, too, would be voting Labour.

Although I put my heart into the job, I was surprised when the Labour Party won. I was sure that we were going to lose because the policies we were publicly advocating were insufficiently radical. We should have *said* that we were going to redistribute the personal wealth of the country through a gifts tax, we should have *said* that we were going to disarm unilaterally, we should have *said* that we were going to make National Savings honest for the small man by paying decent rates of interest on Post Office Savings accounts and by starting a State Unit Trust. I was quite wrong and lost a lot of money to my friends in the City who had been resigned to a Labour victory for some months.

Ivor Richard won the seat at Barons Court from the sitting Conservative member (who just might, if the cookie had crumbled another way, see p. 21 *ante*, have been me), and an American professor has written a book (in which I figure under a pseudonym) giving it as his opinion that this was due to superior Labour organisation in the constituency. Goodness knows what the Tory organisation can have been like, because ours seemed to me to be a complete shambles. Looming in the background the whole time was this lack of money. Leaflets ran out because not enough had been ordered to save money. There were suddenly no envelopes to address because of a shortage of funds earlier in the year. Canvassers could not be deployed in the right places because there was no car to transport them. I was appalled, and thought I could see a future for myself in the party by trying to do something about it.

It was this determination which led me early in 1965 to launch Labour's Golden Prize Clubs. This was a device by which Labour Party supporters signed a banker's order for £1 per month which automatically bought them twenty 1s. (5p) chances in a small lottery held under the provisions of the Betting, Gaming and Lotteries Act, 1963. The proceeds of this monthly lottery were split: 50 per cent in prizes (maximum £100); 40 per cent to the Constituency Labour Party of the member's choice; and 10 per cent in expenses. I found an enthusiastic ally in Alan Clarke, the Barons Court agent. Winston Fletcher handled the advertising; George Tindle (an old colleague from solicitoring days) the legal side; and we recruited an immensely capable part-time secretary, Pamela Barlow, to do the administration. It began with great success as a result of an enthusiastic article by Gerald Kaufman in the *New Statesman* (3 September 1965) and we had signed up 300 or 400 members in a relatively short space of time. For each member it could recruit, a Constituency Labour Party received £4 16s. (£4.80) per annum with no trouble or expense to itself. It was an excellent scheme and is still running. Over the years it has brought in several thousands of pounds to the party. Various administrative bugs were ironed out and Labour Golden Prize Clubs seemed to me in 1965 to be poised for growth in the way in which I had seen the Save and Prosper Group grow in the previous five years.

While I was teaching summer school at Boulder (part of the University of Colorado in the U.S.A.) in July 1965, my office in London received a personal letter for me from the Governor of the Bank of England. Lord Cromer said that he felt it might be useful for the Prime Minister and Chancellor of the Exchequer to meet some leading City personalities and invited me to dine at the Bank later that month. But the date coincided with the last three days of my course, when I was involved in the crucially important (although impossible) job of "grading" my pupils. Despite the majesty of the invitation I was obliged to decline.

When I got back, I wrote a letter of abject apology and detailed explanation to the Bank of England official who was running these dinners as a result of which I was invited again on Wednesday, 13 October. That occasion was the first on which I played a small "walking-on" part on the Great Stage of history (or so I thought).

When I was introduced to Harold Wilson by Lord Cromer, the Prime Minister charmed the wits out of me by saying that he had been hoping to meet me for some time and had tried to get hold of me at Blackpool in the previous week (when I had been visiting the Labour Party Conference with Winston Fletcher trying to promote the Golden Prize Clubs). He wanted to acknowledge that he had lifted his antithesis between "making money" and "earning money" (with which he had made great play during the 1964 general election campaign) straight from my

Tract on Tax Reform. He later acknowledged this most handsomely to the assembled (and distinguished) company. Here I felt was the difference between the amateur and the professional. The amateur might have been briefed to know that I had once written a tract on tax reform: the professional had actually read it and remembered what he had read. My spirits soared into the sky, much aided by the governor's excellent champagne. Then it was Jim Callaghan's turn. Had I thought of getting myself on the List "B" of approved Labour parliamentary candidates? He would be glad to be one of my two sponsors. I over-reached myself by asking him if he thought the Prime Minister would be my other sponsor. Jim seemed slightly put out at this suggestion: I was his protege. So I let that idea drop.

Callaghan was as good as his word and when the application of the Barons Court Constituency Labour Party to have me put on List "B" arrived too late for me to appear on the list before the 1966 general election, he took up my case (in vain) with Sara Barker, the national agent. The list was inexorably closed: and, as she explained, there was no point in my name being put on because all constituency parties had selected their candidates. During that campaign I spoke in various West Country constituencies at the behest of the national agent's department, spending the last week in Meriden (Christopher Rowland's constituency) where I was once again appalled at the lack of any organisation. Christopher hadn't even a reliable map of his constituency. I also met George Brown for the first time. He was to make a speech and then have lunch with us at an hotel in the constituency. On his arrival, he mistook me for a waiter and ordered from me a large tomato juice with Worcestershire sauce in it. He seemed genuinely upset when he discovered his mistake. But I got him his tomato juice, and he remains, to me, something of a hero for his relative straightforwardness as a politician.

It was at about this time that I made what, in retrospect, I see to be a thoroughly wrong-headed decision. There seemed to be an obvious job to be done (and which I flattered myself I could do) in improving the Labour Party's organisation and fund-raising capability. At the back of my mind was a hope that if this fund-raising problem could be cracked, the Labour Party might get itself out of its near total financial dependence on the trades union movement. If every constituency party were to affiliate with 5,000 members (in those days this would have cost about £250 per annum, a not unattainable goal) the constituency section would have more votes than the trades union section at the Annual Conference, which plays such an important part in Labour Party ritual. I do not think I was the only member of the Labour Party who looked forward to a day when the link between the trades unions and the Labour party would be loosened and not strengthened. Although I did not go as far as some of my friends who held the view (and not without some good reasons) that organised labour had been wrong about every big decision it had taken in the preceding century, I was nervous about being perpetually tied to its lead.

Len Williams, the party's general secretary, was reaching the age at which he would retire. He had no obvious successor because Sara Barker was approaching retirement too. If I did my job sufficiently well, I might even have a chance of succeeding him. I consulted Jim Callaghan to ask him if it were on the cards that I might have a chance of becoming general secretary. He made absolutely no promises, but he seemed enthusiastic about the idea. The succession was quite open, he assured me. I definitely got the impression that, other things being equal, I would be his candidate. In retrospect I can see that it was never on the cards at all. Even with his support there was no chance whatever of anyone with my deplorable background getting the job. The only member of the National Executive Committee who told me so from the very outset was Eirene White.

Engineering the move to Transport House proved to be quite easy. Len Williams was under pressure to appoint a full-time fund-raiser, but he thought he could not afford one. A few weeks previously I had been approached by Robert Maxwell with the generous proposal that his National Fund-Raising Foundation should merge with my Golden Prize Clubs (with him as chairman) so that we should not be thought to be competing with one another. I invited Len Williams to the first of many extremely agreeable orgies at the Reform Club and asked his advice about Robert Maxwell's offer. It was not a move he favoured. He was, however, prepared to recommend to the N.E.C. that the Labour Party should sponsor the Golden Prize Clubs on a national basis—and he would be glad to welcome me at Transport House as fund-raising adviser, particularly if I was unpaid. I reported this back to Maxwell and promised that, when safely entrenched in Transport House, I would do my best to bring in his organisation too.

So I took the not inconsiderable decision to abandon my lucrative and prestigious job in the City as managing director of the Save and Prosper Group and move to the humble and unpaid job of fund-raising adviser to the N.E.C. In those days I was a sufficiently important person for the news of my appointment to get a certain amount of good-natured derision in the national press. The *Daily Express* City page featured a cartoon of two City gents walking past a placard announcing my appointment, the one saying to the other: "Wasn't it some chap named Oliver who kept asking for more?" It was not, of course, that I was important, but the institution (Save and Prosper) that I ran which was important. That was why my move was newsworthy.

I started my new job at the beginning of October 1966 as the Labour Party met for its Annual Conference, that year held in Brighton. During the summer holidays I had begun trying to acquire a new persona for myself. I threw away my bowler hat. I discarded my waistcoats (they were becoming uncomfortably confining in any case) and took to wearing V-necked pullovers instead. When I turned up at my first Save and Prosper board meeting as a non-executive director, one of my colleagues flattered me by saying that I looked like a seedy trades union official. It was certainly what I was aiming to look like.

I find it difficult to describe the total difference in *atmosphere* between working in any City office I have ever been in, and working at Transport House. Everybody at Transport House was very nice to me indeed, but in one way or another they were being deprived (or should I say exploited?) in a way which is highlighted by the following incident. On 27 July 1967, the Prime Minister and Mrs Wilson invited all the Transport House staff (including me) to a very pleasant social gathering at No. 10 Downing Street. At an appropriate moment he made a presentation to Miss Selley, the head of the directory department who was retiring having completed forty-eight years' service with the party—fifty years, if the two years were included in which she had worked for its predecessor before the Labour Party was officially constituted. I knew of no commercial organisation or charity which would have dared to give anyone less than £50 for fifty years' service, but the Prime Minister handed her a cheque for £20. After the ceremony was over, I expostulated with him as politely as I could. Harold Wilson quite agreed with me, but he said, the N.E.C. were a mean lot. But, I said to myself, if he couldn't do something about it, who could? As I left No. 10, Alf Richman (one of Wilson's aides) was having a whip-round of the Prime Minister's personal staff to collect enough money to give the attendants a tip. Among those working for the Labour Party I found no one who thought their employer was other than mean. As I was eventually to discover, everyone (not just the Prime Minister) agreed that things were a disgrace, but no one was prepared to try and do anything about it, because there was no hope of achieving anything.

I made up my mind that I was jolly well going to achieve something. I set to work with some confidence and the enthusiastic support of the party's finance officer, Douglas Richards, to expand membership of Labour's Golden Prize Clubs. We arranged with Desmond Hirshfield that his firm, the Labour Party's auditors, should supervise the monthly draw and audit the accounts. Without Douglas Richards's consistent and continuous support throughout my time at Transport House, I should have given up the struggle long before I did. (He used to say that he found it surprising that I stayed the course for so long.)

Douglas was typical of the kind of person whose unacknowledged self-sacrifice in the party's cause was beyond all praise, whose treatment by the party in terms of remuneration and recognition was quite deplorable. I look back with nothing but gratitude for the help which he gave me personally.

I wanted us to start by mounting a national advertising campaign for Golden Prize Club members. It was here that I began for the first time to feel the dead hand of the national agent's department on my project. Walter Brown, their legal expert, took the view that it was illegal to advertise the clubs because it was also advertising the lotteries and the advertising of lotteries was illegal. This was nonsense, said I. We had been through all this before. I was, after all, a solicitor. I had the written opinion of leading counsel, Sam Silkin, Q.C., and of Ivor Richard that although the matter was not wholly free from doubt, on balance the better opinion was that advertising the clubs would not be illegal. Ivor Richards (bless him!) called on the general secretary to reassure him that the weight of opinion was on my side and the N.E.C. could safely go ahead. After all a prosecution would not be the end of the world, particularly as it was unlikely to be successful. But the national agent's department won.

Len Williams decided that to protect the N.E.C. he must get yet another opinion, and Douglas Richards and I went to see Arnold Goodman in his offices just off Fleet Street. My clearest recollection of these conferences with Goodman, apart from his obvious good sense and judgment, is of a ceaseless string of telephone calls. He seemed to like doing two things at once, which was slightly disconcerting to his clients. When the telephonist was firmly told by one of his assistants not to put through any more calls, the great man seemed deprived and unhappy. Goodman himself seemed disposed to take my line, but then he called in one of his partners and an assistant who took Walter Brown's line. I could not fathom *why* they should choose to dispute leading counsel's opinion when it accorded with their client's wishes. They agreed to let us have their views in writing and, in the end, Messrs Goodman, Derrick and Co. counselled caution—the Walter Brown line.

To this day I cannot understand how Alf Richman was the first journalist to become aware of our little local legal difficulties and to write about them in the press, which predictably refused thereafter to accept our advertising. But I have my suspicions!

This was a serious but not, I thought, insuperable blow to the growth of the Golden Prize Clubs. Without advertising we could still circularise all local Labour Parties and ask them to push the plan. This we did, offering to find a speaker to describe how it worked and to give advice on how to recruit members. In this way we hoped that the word would spread gradually, and that as the success of the clubs was established, more and more constituency parties would adopt the scheme.

It did not happen this way. There was very little response from local Labour Parties to the circular. There were many reasons for this. It was partly the inefficiency and ineffectiveness of local Labour Parties in general. It was partly the general distrust and contempt in which Transport House was held by the Labour Party in the country at large. (I never in all my years in the Labour Party, met a single member—from the Leader downwards—who had a good word to say for Transport House.) But it was due also to a more deep-seated fault in the Labour organisation, which could only be corrected, I thought, by far more radical reforms. It was to these that I proceeded to address my attention.

There were basically two sorts of C.L.P. from the fund-raising point of view. One sort had a modest income. In those days there were about 200 full-time agents employed by this sort of constituency party, but they already had their fund-raising schemes—it might be a conventional 1s. (5p) a week tote, or it might be a "Hundred Club" (another form of lottery) or it might be a bingo hall. This sort was not interested in the Golden Prize Clubs because either they didn't need the income, or they were afraid that it would channel money away from their own schemes. It was in vain for me to point out that a local party was legally allowed to make no more money from its own tote than it could make from getting its members to join the Golden Prize Clubs (and we would be doing their administration for them for nothing) because they did not want to let the thing out of their own hands. My suspicion was (and still is) that many of these local totes (not all) did not adhere as closely to the law as they should have done, and that quite a few persons were making a nice little personal fiddle from them, on the side.

The other sort of local Labour Party had virtually no income, no paid agent and very little organisation. These could be split into two categories. Those which were run by a devoted band of brothers and sisters who were idealistic socialists, uninterested in (and suspicious of) money and organisation. They were usually in safe Tory seats. In the safe Labour seats were the other category. They were run by a clique of people who often composed the ruling party on the local authority and had strong trades union connections. The last thing such a clique wanted was an increase in party membership and activity. If they wanted money for an election, they had a whip-round of their members and the trades unions, and raised all they wanted but no more.

So the Constituency Labour Parties as a whole were no use as retail outlets for fund-raising schemes. If the aim was to raise significant sums of money one would have to go "over their heads" and attract a wider range of Labour supporter. The trouble was that far too many people in the Labour Party nationally liked it in exactly the parlous administrative and financial condition it was in. The people at the top, who could have done something about it, had reached their present eminences because they had been able to play on these weaknesses. So they had no incentive or desire to get it changed. When I first went to the organisation sub-committee of the N.E.C. to outline methods by which money could be raised otherwise than from the trades unions, one of the older members voiced a thought which other trades unionists would be quite frank with me about in private—that they wanted the Labour Party's financial dependence on the trades unions to stay just as it was. It gave them the sort of political leverage they wanted at the Conference, and they had no wish to see that leverage slipping away to anyone else.

After a bit I made up my mind that I had come to the wrong place and that if an improvement was to be achieved in the Labour Party's organisation I should go to Congress House. But George Woodcock, who had lunch with us at Save and Prosper on 20 April 1967, made it quite clear that he was anxious to keep the T.U.C. out of Labour Party affairs as far as he could; and later on, still, after lobbying Vic Feather at Harry Nicholas's instigation, I found that it was hopeless to expect help from that quarter. Congress House had made a decision that the trades union members of the N.E.C. were not to act as a caucus. So, like Harold Wilson, they had made a positive decision not to play any part in the organisation of the party. Nobody was in the least interested. The career politicians on the N.E.C. were interested in Transport House only in so far as it could further their ambitions in the House of Commons; the trades union members were interested in the N.E.C. only in so far as it would enable them to get to the Number One job in their own unions when they hoped to be elected to the general council of the T.U.C. and (by tradition) would resign from the N.E.C. Transport House was nobody's baby.

In the early part of 1967, I submitted a paper proposing a number of changes (primarily the creation of a national register of members of the party) in evidence to a committee into party organisation which had been set up under the chairmanship of one of the trades union N.E.C. members, Willie Simpson. Len Williams saw it and said that I had exceeded my brief which was confined to fund-raising. But, as I had explained to him on previous occasions, it was not possible to improve fund-raising without improving the organisation, and he let the document go forward. I sent a copy to Callaghan and went to see him at 9.45 a.m. on Friday, 17 March. I surmised that, understandably, he had not had time to read my paper, but he said (*inter alia*) that he had mentioned my name to the Prime Minister as a possible next general secretary and that he had not turned it down flat. Jim said that he thought he had the treasurership of the party in the bag at the next Conference and hoped that he would then be in a better position to assist me.

I still wanted to prove to the national agent's department that the Golden Prize Clubs would work. I was not prepared at that stage to throw in my hand. Jim Callaghan spoke at a Golden Prize Club meeting during the Party Conference in Scarborough on the evening of Thursday 5 October. At that meeting a Labour parliamentary candidate in 1966 called Ron Truman got up and made a heart-warming speech about the scheme—in which he confessed he had an interest because he had just won a £100 prize. He turned out to be an insurance company official and an exceedingly gifted salesman. With his help and a grant from the N.E.C (engineered for us by the new treasurer) we undertook to take a team of paid canvassers to any constituency selected by the national agent's department and show them that, given the will, the members could be enrolled. Sara Barker selected Rugby; and with the enthusiastic support of Bill Price, the sitting member, a team of six of us moved into Rugby from 3 until 11 February 1968. It was a highly professional operation under Ron's leadership and out of 300 calls, 98 new Golden Prize members were signed up (see *Labour Organiser*, April 1968). This represented an annual income of £470 to the Rugby Constituency Labour Party, and for a fortnight's effort was not to be sneezed at. It could be done. But nobody wanted to know.

No other party again offered us this sort of co-operation. In fairness to the national agent's department it has to be said that doing something for the Rugby party did not induce the Rugby party to do anything for Transport House. It remained in arrears on its affiliation fees for some years. But I do not think I am being unfair in pinning at least part of the blame for my total inability to get anything done, fairly and squarely on the shoulders of the national agent's department. The department ran many potential agents training courses sponsored (at considerable expense) by the N.E.C. After repeated requests I was allowed on one occasion only to address such a course for a quarter of an hour at the end of a two-hour session in which

Walter Brown had spent the first one and a half hours outlining what schemes could not be done in the way of fund-raising because they were against the law. I was never asked again. A refresher course for full-time agents was held each year at Beatrice Webb House. There was usually (if not always) a session on fund-raising. As the party's full-time fund-raiser, I was never-once invited to address the course. I only came to know of its existence because I was told of it in 1970 by the chairman of the National Union of Labour Organisers. I got on personally quite amicably with Sara Barker, Reg Underhill and their team. Later, I was on perfectly amicable terms with Sara's successor, the amiable extroverted Ron Hayward. I don't blame them for wanting to thwart my plans to transform the national agent's department into a head office running a species of national direct sales force. They would have been quite unable to fill what would have been quite a different rôle. But it became quite clear to me (as it had been all along to Douglas Richards) that they did not want me to succeed. In the end they won, and I lost.

I did not confine my efforts to the Golden Prize Clubs. After lengthy negotiations we eventually absorbed what there was of Robert Maxwell's National Fund-Raising Foundation (i.e. one person, Bryan Barnard) into Transport House and I gave a little luncheon party at the Reform Club for Maxwell at which Jim Callaghan made a speech. At a Northern Home Counties Regional agents' conference I met Dr Colin Phipps who, as secretary and agent of the Windsor party, had had considerable success in turning that party's hall to financial advantage. Colin Phipps was someone of first-rate ability and we became close friends and associates in a common aim to get the Labour Party run on reasonably business-like lines. (In 1974 he was elected M.P. for Dudley West.) Between us we persuaded the N.E.C. to start a Labour Party Property Company (of which he became first managing director) with the object of giving advice to local labour parties on how best to exploit their real estate. In some instances, Labour halls were slipping out of the Labour Party's control altogether owing to deficiencies in title. We calculated that over the country as a whole, local Labour parties owned property worth several millions of pounds and this, if it could be properly organised, could be used as a base from which to assist other parties who had no accommodation at all.

I spent a great deal of time, too, in trying to crack the Labour Party Social Club problem: how to organise a club in such a way that the social activities did not, in the end, conflict with the political activities, causing a rift in the party's supporters which defeated the object of the whole enterprise. In the end, Paul Carmody, the regional organiser in Lancashire and Cheshire, persuaded me that it could not be done. Another avenue, first suggested by Gwyn Morgan, the head of the overseas department at Transport House, who had made profitable use of the idea when he was secretary of the National Union of Students, was the possibility of being able to offer Labour Party supporters cheap holidays abroad sponsored by fraternal political parties in countries round the Mediterranean. Galleon Holidays (as the Workers Travel Association had recently been renamed) seemed an ideal body to co-operate with us on this venture: and with the general secretary's support Douglas Richards and I called on Jack Jones (who was then treasurer of Galleon) to see if anything could be arranged. Promises were made but no arrangement was ever finalised because there was nothing we at Transport House could offer firmly as our part of the bargain.

In 1968 came the news that Len Williams was retiring early to become the Governor and Commander-in-Chief in Mauritius. I sought and gained an interview with Jim Callaghan at the Home Office on 15 February 1968 to ask his advice on how best to further my candidature for the succession. I was completely taken aback to discover that I no longer had his support—at that moment, he told me, Willie Simpson would get the job if he wanted it. I told Jim that I had been spending my time at Transport House trying not to make enemies, and that I thought I had been successful in this negative aim. "A pity you haven't picked up a few friends," he said jovially. Although I could quite understand that he should change his mind about my candidature, I found it hard to forgive him for not having told me so rather earlier on. But, after all, he had been a Cabinet Minister and a very busy man. He had had better things to do, and I suppose I couldn't complain.

I did not throw in my hand. The party was in the most appalling financial and organisational mess, and it was crucially important for the next general secretary to devote himself to these problems and for him not to involve himself in politics. Tony Benn seemed enthusiastic and remarked that to do it properly I should be made a peer (about which I was then less than enthusiastic because I still hoped, one day, to get into the Commons). As is now a matter of history, when the post was advertised, the short list (on which my name did *not* appear) was scrapped and the job was given to Harry Nicholas, the assistant general secretary of the Transport and General Workers' Union in a deal which made obvious political sense. The N.E.C. announced that it was going to create a new appointment of assistant general secretary, but at a party soon after the announcement both Callaghan and Eirene White told me that there was no point in my hoping to get that job because it had been tailor-made for Gwyn Morgan. It was another kick in the teeth, but I was not to be lightly put off.

CHAPTER FIVE

I SCORE A DUCK

WHEN Len Williams left Transport House I received the one and only firm offer of a job of any sort (even to serve on a Government committee) I received at the hands of the Labour Government during the whole period of Mr Wilson's various administrations. Len asked me if I would like to become his A.D.C. in his new capacity as Governor-General of Mauritius. He knew I wanted time to develop my Ph.D. thesis into a book, and thought the job would be idle enough to give me the necessary scope. I was touched and flattered, but I did not accept.

What concerned me, as I wrote in an article for the *New Statesman* which Paul Johnson rejected (23 July 1968), was the complete misunderstanding evinced by all the newspapers about the problems which would face Harry Nicholas when he took Len's place after the Conference. They spoke as if his job was to enthuse the "grass-roots" of the Labour Party with the spirit to work for the Government. The outstanding fact was not that the organisation was bad, but that it was non-existent in two-thirds of the country. Given an organisation like this, Keir Hardie himself could not have enthused the grass-roots. This involved communication, and if the Prime Minister and his colleagues could not get to the grass-roots with the media available to them, what hope, for Heaven's sake, had the bloke running "the penny-farthing machine" (as Harold Wilson had dubbed it in 1955)? The Conference and the National Executive Committee was being grossly misled if it was deluded into supposing that anyone in the office of general secretary, given the then state of the party's organisation, was within several years march of being able to be a "second focus of power" within the party.

The general secretary's proper job was to see that the party organisation did the humdrum political jobs like keeping reliable registers of supporters, collecting subscriptions and money, marking Registers of Electors, and delivering the votes at elections. If Transport House did not get that done, nobody else would. They were failing at that time because of the system by which each C.L.P. was an autonomous employer of labour and engaged its own organiser. As a result of this system not only were organisers shamefully underpaid, but they were at the mercy of the lowest common denominator of their constituency party. There was no promotion structure at all, and, not surprisingly, they were a dwindling body.

The vital task of the next general secretary was to create a national agency service on the right lines. He had to insist on very much better conditions of employment for organisers, and to persuade local parties to allow them to be responsible both for pay and discipline to the regional organisers. What brought me close to despair about the Labour Party was that nobody in power seemed to recognise that the humdrum political jobs needed to be properly done by someone, and so many of our most perceptive political commentators seemed oblivious of the fact that it needed to be done at all.

These were my thoughts but I determined to give it one more try in the hope that I could work through the new general secretary. I did not find Harry Nicholas unreceptive to these ideas. I saw him very often and he was sympathetic. We became firm friends. He tried (he told me) to get the Prime Minister to make me a peer at the time of the 1970 dissolution. Nevertheless, I was allowed no hand at all in setting up the new national agency service. This was started off on precisely the wrong lines. Instead of its members being made the employees of Transport House and subject, exclusively, to the authority of the regional organisers, they remained the employees of the Constituency Labour Party to whom they were appointed (and by whom they were selected) and Transport House's only involvement was an undertaking to foot most of the bill. As any child could have predicted, the Constituency Labour Party involved then turned over in bed and no longer made any serious effort to raise funds or organise themselves properly.

It was all very disappointing. There was nothing I could do for the time being. I helped Harry Nicholas with his Fighting Fivers Fund. Douglas Richards and I designed the form of banker's order for enabling members' subscriptions to the party to be paid by a method which did not involve the absurdly inefficient 1s. (5p) per month collection. I also tried (and failed) to get other people at Transport House involved in subscribing to the blueprint on how the party should be reorganised. This was the document which was eventually published as a part of *Fabian Tract 407* and which I look upon (although it was never used) as one of my *opera minora*. I could get no one else to put their name to it, not even Douglas Richards, although he supported nearly every recommendation that I made.

At about this time, for some reason that I do not understand (because I had not sought the job), I found myself a member of the committee of the Reform Club. Another member was Frank Figgures and I remember, after one committee meeting, walking with him through St James's Park, he on his way back to the Treasury, I on my way back to Transport House, and discussing the affairs of the moment, when he ended the conversation by saying: "But don't you see? *Nobody* has any positive power nowadays?" Coming from a Treasury mandarin this was a very remarkable admission. I did not believe him at that time. But with more experience behind me, I would now concede that he was much nearer the truth than I was. (Certainly neither of us, despite determined efforts, had the least effect on the running of the Reform, which remained firmly attached to its nineteenth-century habits.)

For the moment I turned my hand to other things. The first Wilson Government was a great *political* disappointment to nearly all its supporters. During his premiership Harold Macmillan had taken the Conservatives Party so far to the Left that there was no way in which Gaitskell could outflank him, now Wilson seemed intent on the same manoeuvre in reverse.

There was no discernible radicalism in its outlook. I looked upon the 1965 Finance Act (which introduced the corporation and capital gains taxes) as an unmitigated political disaster—not because the reforms were necessarily wrong-headed (although I personally thought they were) but because they created an administrative log-jam in the accountancy profession and the Inland Revenue which, for several years, prevented the introduction of the taxes on capital which people of my cast of mind thought crucial. If any one person is to be blamed for this, I blame Nicholas Kaldor. To my mind, because I look upon the way taxes are raised as one of the (if not the most) important tasks of central government, he is the real villain of the 1964–70 Labour Government. Wise politicians (as I have suggested) are only brokers of other people's ideas. They cannot afford to run their own ideas because they become too involved. I do not blame Jim Callaghan for the 1965 Finance Act, I blame the authors of the Minority Report of the Millard Tucker Commission. And why the Prime Minister and his Chancellor of the Exchequer paid any attention to Nicholas Kaldor I shall never be able to fathom. We were later to collaborate in a different political campaign and I (like everyone else who has met him) fell a victim to his charm, and became devoted to him as a person. No doubt he was also trying (at this time) to persuade the government to do the correct thing in devaluing the pound. All honour to him for that. But as their adviser on taxation matters he was a disaster.

The classical definition of a good-looking horse is "one with many good, few indifferent, and no bad points". The same definition would go for Prime Ministers, and (to my mind) Wilson's outstandingly bad point was that he made a series of lousy appointments. Moreover, it was not for lack of good candidates. In the House of Commons he seemed to me to have an innate fear of anyone who was any good at all, unless he was obliged to take them in for political reasons. Perhaps there were better reasons than the public knew about, but otherwise his first major reshuffle could only be explained on the basis that he was determined to see that all the able people under fifty years old (and consequently an eventual threat to him) were demoted. Richard Marsh's dismissal is inexplicable on any other grounds.

The whole Government was riddled with economists. The present state of the discipline called "economics" gives me the creeps. It is in the same condition as was moral philosophy at the time of J. S. Mill and as late as G. E. Moore. Mill and Moore genuinely felt that, as philosophers, they had a special insight into how one ought to behave. Moral philosophers have become wiser than that nowadays, and you will not find a respectable one who is so arrogant. But academic economists today still seem genuinely to feel that as a result of their discipline, they have a special insight in telling governments how to behave in the economic field. The real trouble with Keynes was that he was such a successful man of affairs that simple people came to believe that there was a special magic in his academic discipline. There was and is none.

My proposals for tax reform had been out of the public's eye for too long. I persuaded Tom Ponsonby (the new secretary of the Fabian Society) to reopen the Fabian Society's consideration of my original manuscript on tax reform and I produced a re-write which, although basically the same, included a proposal for a wealth tax together with two draft Bills (settled by my friend Ralph Instone), one to introduce what (at his suggestion) I now called a Gratuitous Enrichment Tax (not Fortuitous Enrichment Tax), and the other a mild annual Wealth Tax on net capital assets in excess of £50,000.

It took me two years (from the beginning of 1967 to the end of 1968) to get the Fabian Society's agreement to my text. I never discovered the identity of my most persistent critic, but he, and some of the other Fabian readers (Peter Townsend was one), objected to the "shrill" way in which I attacked the concept of surtax on the higher income brackets, and insisted that these confiscatory rates of tax on income should be abolished at the same time as the new taxes on capital were imposed. But I held to my ground and, in the end, I was allowed to have my way.

But I was also forced to remove from my text one of the new ideas which I had introduced into my *Tract*, and which I still think is a valuable pointer to future thinking on this subject. "Pensions," I had written, "are something for which a well-ordered society should have no place. Perhaps at the moment (most jobs being what they are) they are a necessary evil. But the ideal at which national policy should be aimed is the abolition of all pensions. Jobs ought to be made so absorbingly interesting that their occupants should be joyfully in their employment and doing a good job of work at age eighty (like some recent holders of high judicial office)." I went on to outline some of the alterations in the tax code which would be required to foster such a development. The only piece of machinery which is needed to make this sort of ideal feasible is some sort of automatic device to ease people out of the top jobs in any business or other institutions after they have been doing it for a certain maximum number of years (from three to seven depending on the institution) irrespective of their age.

My Fabian pamphlet, *The Case for Capital Taxes* (No. 388), was published at the end of 1968. I am not as proud of it as I am of my *Tract*. In the first place I had had to compromise with my most persistent critic, and the chart (which I called the cornerstone of my argument) which displayed the staggering inequalities of wealth in Great Britain turned out to have been mistakenly conceived (in all good faith) by its author (not me). None the less (and Terry Pitt, the head of the research department at Transport House, flattered me by confirming this on one occasion) it was, I believe, moderately influential. The publication of the pamphlet generated a flurry of invitations to speak, and I voiced my disappointment at the Labour Party's tax record to a group of Labour Members of the House of Commons organised by Alistair Macdonald (M.P. for Chislehurst) on 28 April 1969 (I remember Joel Barnett saying that my proposals were too radical and the country would not stand for them—it did not like change); to the Chelsea Constituency Labour Party (of which I was shortly to become a member) on 3 June 1969; to the

Cambridge University Fabian Society on 14 October 1969; and to the Blue Ribbon Club at Oxford on 26 January 1970. It was at Cambridge I discovered how old I had become. On questioning the audience, I discovered that none of them had been born by the time I had come down from the university—a moment which seemed but yesterday to me.

I was still concentrating my medium-term ambitions on trying to do something about the Labour Party's organisation, but I felt that I could afford to wait. The organisation was getting worse as more and more constituencies could no longer afford a full-time agent, or as the latter moved to other more rewarding jobs. The "profit" which Len Williams was able proudly to proclaim after each election over which he presided, would not for ever go on lasting out the expense of keeping up Transport House throughout the period between elections. Then the party would go bust, and things might start to happen.

I myself made up my mind that I would soldier on at Transport House until the next general election. If the party lost, then people stronger than myself would, I felt sure, be pressing for a full-scale inquiry (like that conducted by Harold Wilson in the 1950s) into the shameful state of its organisation. If it won, then I would see if I could not get a job of some sort in the Government machine connected with taxation where I might be able to influence it towards my reforms. Meanwhile, I lost no opportunity of trying to propagate my views. Jim Callaghan, Denis Healey, Walter Padley, Fred Mulley, Shirley Williams, Eirene White—any member of the N.E.C. I thought I could suborn were sent copies of my blueprint—and I often reinforced my intellectual argument with what I hoped was judicious hospitality. By the end the only member of the Labour Party to whom I owed hospitality (rather than the other way round) was Roy Jenkins, who gave me a delightful lunch at Brooks's. He appeared to think my case overwhelming. I have tried very hard, without success, to repay the hospitality.

After the Labour Party's defeat in May 1970, I redoubled my efforts. I started badgering Jim Callaghan (as party treasurer) by letter, and Harry Nicholas by argument, pressing them to insist that my blueprint on the party organisation be received by the appropriate N.E.C. committee. As I wrote to Callaghan in a letter dated 15 July 1970, I had for over six months been trying to get it considered (not necessarily approved) by the organisation sub-committee of the N.E.C.—without any success. But he was too much involved in other things to see me. As Reg Underhill (the assistant national agent) explained to me with his usual engaging candour, my thesis was totally impractical, but it was argued in such a way that people who didn't know anything about it (like the N.E.C.) might think it worth a try, and that would be disastrous. After another attempt on my part to see him, Callaghan wrote to me on 14 September to say he was sorry our last appointment had had to be cancelled, but he hoped that Harry Nicholas was going to fix up a further meeting before Conference, when we could have a talk about organisation and other matters. I wrote back on 17 September to say that I had more or less come to the conclusion that, as things stood, there was no job for me to do at Transport House and I had better confess to failure and pack it in. No meeting was arranged.

I thought (mistakingly it seems) I had obtained a pledge from Harry Nicholas that some sort of inquiry would be announced during the Party Conference when the defeated Government met its supporters in Blackpool. If the party was going to carry on in the same old way, then I was just wasting my time. It was in this sort of mood that I caught the train from Euston on Saturday, 26 September. Conference was its usual boozy, exciting self, but when, after the private session on Tuesday, it looked as if the organisation issue were being ducked again, I sent my draft letter of resignation to Harry Nicholas for his comments and said I intended to publish it. No murmur reached me from the general secretary's suite, so I delivered the letter on Friday, 2 October. In it I reiterated, at the risk of being tiresome, that my job as the party's fund-raising adviser could not be performed effectively in the then state of the party's organisation in the country. I had resisted the impulse to resign before on his assurance that a high-level inquiry was to be instigated at the 1970 Conference. No inquiry had been forthcoming, and I could see no point whatever in my carrying on. But I promised that my decision to leave Transport House would not prevent me trying to do anything I could to help. In the event, Harry asked me to remain on the boards of the property company and the company running the Golden Prize Clubs.

My resignation was reported in some newspapers (and to my great pride mentioned in the *Times* leading article on 26 November 1970) but not to the same extent as my move to Transport House had been reported four years earlier. Having no institution behind me I was a less important person. The Labour Party as a whole took not the slightest notice.

In June 1971 the Fabian Society published my blueprint on how the party should be reorganised in a symposium entitled *The Labour Party*: *an organisational study* (Tract 407, edited by Inigo Bing). In it I forecast (as indeed Douglas Richards had forecast to the N.E.C.) that the party's annual deficit would rise from £153,000 in 1971 to an estimated £398,000 in 1975. No foreseeable "profits" on running general elections could cope with that sort of deficit. I ended: "The time has come for action. Many of us feel that there is something degrading about belonging to a party which aspires to run the country, but is manifestly incapable of conducting its own affairs with anything which resembles competence." The intellectual case seemed to me to be overwhelming. But Alan Watkins published a perceptive piece in the *New Statesman* (11 June 1971) saying that I was quite wrong and trying to turn the Labour Party into something more like the Conservative Party than it was already, that for all practical purposes the Labour Party had all the funds it needed and that its members didn't want to be involved in politics, they simply wanted to be associated with the party's policies when these had been generated. He may well have been right.

When Harry Nicholas retired, I wrote to Tony Benn, the chairman of the party, asking if there was any point in my applying for the general secretary's job and received a cordial letter back which was so inscrutably ambiguous that I thought there would be no harm in having a bash. So I applied on 15 March 1972, simultaneously sending all twenty-eight members of the N.E.C. a copy of the Fabian Tract and complaining that after four years at Transport House I had not even been able to get my views considered. To my surprise, I was one of the five applicants who were short-listed for the job. I did not really believe the reports in *The Times* and *Guardian* to this effect, until *Labour Weekly* rang me up and asked for my photograph. In typical Transport House fashion it was two days before I received the official intimation from Bert Williams, the administrative officer, that I was to appear at Transport House at 11 a.m. on Wednesday, 29 March. The other candidates were Gwyn Morgan (the then assitant general secretary), Ron Hayward and Reg Underhill from the national agent's department, and Dick Clements (editor of *Tribune*, and the candidate of the Left).

I arrived to be told that interviews were running late and that it would be nice if I came back in forty minutes. So I walked across Lambeth Bridge to calm my nerves and arrived back at 11.30 to be told that I was late but that Reg Underhill had filled my spot. Soon afterwards I went in, and did my best to answer the four questions which Tony Benn asked us all, and then I was out again to a reassuring nod from Jim Callaghan. Some members of the N.E.C. told me afterwards that no one paid the least attention to what any of the candidates said in their interviews having all made up their minds beforehand.

The five candidates retired to the general secretary's room at five minutes before noon. By 12.45, Ron Hayward and Reg Underhill had come to the conclusion that the N.E.C. had decided not to select but to look for another candidate. I remember Reg Underhill complaining jokingly that in politics it did not pay to conform. There was Michael Tippett, who had been so far to the Left that he had nearly been kicked out of the Labour Party, being knighted and given the Order of Merit, whereas he (Reg), who had always towed the line, was still plain Mr Underhill.

The old pros were wrong. At 1.15, Tony Benn and Harry Nicholas came into the room to say that Ron Hayward had been elected on the fourth ballot by the chairman's casting vote. Ron Hayward went upstairs to receive the congratulations of the committee. Gwyn Morgan retired up to his room to nurse a broken spirit and Reg, Dick Clements and I repaired to the Marquis of Granby for a drink. On the other side of the bar, hidden in the gloom, we saw a very dispirited Walter Padley. That afternoon Douglas Richards rang me up to say that the voting on the first ballot had been Morgan 14, Hayward 11, Clements 2, Underhill 1, and that Stutchbury had scored a duck. On the second and subsequent ballots Morgan and Hayward had each got 14 votes. Somebody was clearly trying to tell me something.

I continued to help Transport House in any way they asked me but I began to be frightened that things were not as they should have been when on 28 December 1973 I received, by recorded delivery, a final notice from the Department of Trade and Industry saying that as a director of Labour Party Properties Limited I should know that its annual returns for 1971 and 1972 had not been filed and that unless something was done within fourteen days the matter would be referred to the solicitor for the Department. This was cleared up but then in May 1974 I was involved in another misunderstanding. It became clear to me (as I wrote to the general secretary on 5 June) that Transport House could not be trusted to supply the residual minimum of competence which was needed to run the businesses which the boards I was on (the Golden Prize Clubs and the property company) were supposed to supervise. So I resigned. Ron Hayward wrote me a nice letter on 26 July, thanking me for what I had done for the party. That was the end of eight years' effort. The result was total failure.

So I gave up banging my head against a brick wall, but I am left with a classical dilemma about organisation to which I can find no solution. It can be put most neatly as follows: "If organisation matters, then there is no future for the Labour

Party. But it is false that there is no future for the Labour Party, therefore (by the *modus tollendo tollens*) it is false that organisation matters. But it is true that organisation matters." Which horn will emerge as victor? My money goes on the betting that organisation matters.

In retrospect it would have been nice if one of the members of the N.E.C. who had been encouraging me to stick at my thankless job over the years, had broken that duck, by voting for me on the first ballot. But there it was, they hadn't. I must confess that nowadays I look on with a certain secret joy when I see the organisation getting worse (in 1976 there were fewer than 100 agents) and the Labour Government in deep trouble with the N.E.C. and the party organisation in the country. If some of the Labour leaders, at some time, had made common cause with some of the people at Transport House who wanted to see the place changed, then all this nonsense need not have happened. But they were too short-sighted and now they are reaping a harvest which they richly deserve.

CHAPTER SIX

RECONNAISSANCES LEADING NOWHERE

UNTIL my resignation from the job as fund-raiser at Transport House in 1970, although I was unpaid, in accordance with the conditions of service of paid Labour organisers, I had not sought to get myself adopted as a parliamentary (or indeed any other sort of) candidate; although my constituency party had proposed me for it, I was not on List "B". I now had my name put back on the list and actively pursued a parliamentary candidature by writing to all the regional organisers I knew and generally engaging in the highly distasteful business of trying to sell myself to groups of Labour Party activists.

The uninitiated should know that to be exposed to the electorate as a Labour candidate in a constituency, an aspirant has, first, to be nominated by one of the ward parties or affiliated organisation; next to be short-listed by the executive committee and then the general committee of the C.L.P.; next to be selected at a selection conference; and finally his candidature must be endorsed by the N.E.C. To pass the first hurdle (which is statistically the most difficult) can involve attending on a number of ward (or affiliated organisation) private selection conferences. I remember a long selection process at Norwich South in which my name was short-listed by the executive committee but then removed by the general committee. The same thing happened to me at Burton-on-Trent. I tried very hard (perhaps too hard) at Ipswich throughout the summer of 1971, but only just managed to get myself nominated (by the Young Socialists) and I was not short-listed. My only success in reaching a short list was at Ilford North. There at the selection conference on 2 March 1972, I was beaten into third place by Millie Miller (the present M.P.) and

Gladys Dimson, who was a prominent member of the G.L.C.

This was the nearest I was ever to get to a seat on the Labour benches of the House of Commons. I look back with a kind of half-embarrassed, half-amused shudder at the speech (it was always much the same speech) I used to make at those selection conferences. It was largely written for me by the admirable Dr Colin Phipps, who was a notable success at selection conferences himself. He had so extensive a practice in advising people on their selection conference technique, that the regional organisers (who have to attend all final selection conferences to see fair play) could detect a Phipps man from the rest by the sort of balderdash that boomed across the hall. My speech ended up: "I believe an M.P. must be three things to his constituents. He must be their servant, their leader and their friend. I would hope to be all three to you, Comrades. Thank you very much for inviting me here tonight."

I don't think it was the speech's fault that I couldn't get myself selected and I am grateful to Colin for all the help he gave me. The fault was in me and my background, which I could not conceal. In the end, as I learnt in my days as a Conservative candidate, political decisions are made somewhere closer to the stomach than the head. The kind of delegates who assembled for Labour selection conferences very properly suspected that, when the crunch came, I should look after my own, and not theirs. Many of them may even have held old-fashioned Marxist beliefs about the inevitability of the revolution. I was and am unashamedly a law-and-order man. They didn't like what they saw of me, and who was to blame them?

So that the full account of my venality may be on record, I must wind up my account of my efforts to get into Parliament by confessing that on 28 April 1974, I wrote to the Prime Minister (then, once again, Harold Wilson) reminding him that Lord Longford (who was then the Leader of the House of Lords) had cast a fly over me in 1967 to see if I wanted to become a life peer. It had happened at a splendid party given by Nigel and Vanessa Lawson at their house in Hyde Park Gate on 27 July that year.

Longford had told me (as Harold had told me himself that same day) that my name was being bandied about as a possibility, and tried fairly hard to persuade me that it was an agreeable and influential life—but I resisted. Longford eventually gave up, laughed and said: "If you change your mind come and let me know. But, of course, I cannot promise I shall be able to do anything about it then." As I wrote to the Prime Minister: "At the time I was not interested because I hoped to get into the House of Commons. But now I am forty-seven and too old to hope to make much of a mark in the Commons even if I can get myself selected for a winnable seat, which seems unlikely. I know you have long queues of Labour worthies who are hoping that you will send them to the House of Lords. I am just writing to say that I hope my name will not be rejected solely on the grounds that I refused last time."

The Prime Minister replied on 2 May saying that he did appreciate my writing to him. There was a long queue and very many recommendations and, as I would know, the Chief Whip kept a list. He would certainly have a word with him so that every consideration could be given to it again. And that was the last that I heard. It will be apparent that in 1974 I was still up for sale to the Establishment. But I never reached my goal. Harold Wilson's subsequent appointments to the House of Lords seem to me to have made the case for its abolition well-nigh unanswerable.

Another cause close to my heart was the importance of getting the Labour Party committed to a gifts and a wealth tax. Both were proposed in the Labour Party's *Agenda for a Generation* in 1969 and by the T.U.C. in the same year, but not included in the 1970 general election manifesto. In 1971, the Conservative Government published a Green Paper: *Taxation of Capital on Death*: A possible Inheritance Tax in place of Estate Duty (Cmnd. 4930). At that time I was vice-chairman of John Gilbert's Labour Economic Finance and Taxation Association (L.E.F.T.A.) and wrote for them their first pamphlet (but my third) on this topic: *The Case against an Inheritance Tax*. It was inaptly named because I was not against a tax on inheritance as such, but just against the tax proposed by the Conservative Government. I was against the Green Paper "for it confines itself to considering ways in which capital can be taxed on death. The fact is that we all know that death will eventually catch up with us and can consequently take steps to rid ourselves of capital (if we are lucky enough to have any) as death approaches. Further, we can arrange for our beneficiaries to insure themselves against the possibility that death should steal upon us unawares.

"The real criticism of the present estate duty is the *fourth* criticism given in the Green Paper: it is far too easy to avoid. Estate duty, as Labour party spokesmen never tire of affirming, is a voluntary tax. The knock-down argument against an inheritance tax to replace estate duty is that it must, by its very nature, suffer from the same defect. As with estate duty, an inheritance tax will only be borne by beneficiaries whose benefactors are too misanthropic, patriotic, absent-minded, indolent or downright unlucky not to have taken steps to avoid the tax *long* before they die. Any period for the inclusion of gifts *inter vivos* will not be enough because the unit of enrichment nowadays is not the individual person, but the family (in which no one has an interest which is inherited on death). By dint of family trusts, family companies, family partnerships, family clubs, family housing associations, family charities, etc. there is no longer any need for an ingenious benefactor to make any gifts at all himself. He takes trouble to own as little capital as he can himself, and simply arranges for one of these family institutions to do the giving.

"This is why it is the gifts tax which should be the first on the list of Labour priorities. It is crucially important that it should be on the statute book *before* (or better still, but impracticably, *simultaneously with*) the wealth tax. If a wealth tax antedates the gifts tax, your rich man will take trouble to give away as much as he can manage before the gifts tax is on the statute book. So the door will have been closed after the horse has bolted for yet another generation . . .

"Why a promise to introduce a gifts tax and a wealth tax was not included in the 1970 general election manifesto is something of a mystery. But we have it on George Brown's authority that anyway a wealth tax was in some early drafts . . . Let us have no nonsense like this next time. The party should nail to the masthead—first, on top, a gifts tax; and, second, a wealth tax. Both necessary, but in that order. A firm resolution to this effect at the Conference one year would do no harm."

I also became a member of a capital taxation working party of the finance and economic affairs sub-committee of the N.E.C. which met throughout 1973 under Denis Healey's chairmanship. John Gilbert, Joel Barnett, Nicholas Kaldor and A. B. Atkinson were also members. When Denis Healey's first Budget in 1974 contained proposals for a gifts tax (with the promise of a wealth tax to come) I was overjoyed. I wrote to him congratulating him on being wise enough to make the tax chargeable from the date of his statement. I went on to offer any assistance I could give him in any humble, unpaid, unacknowledged capacity in the back rooms on the projects of which, I added, I had made something of a speciality for the previous fifteen years. He brushed me off with a charming reply saying what a pity it would be if my "immense knowledge" could not be used.

When the detailed proposals for the Capital Transfer Tax (C.T.T.) came to be published, I was dismayed to discover that it was proposed to assess the tax on the *donor* rather than the *donee*. John Gilbert had been appointed financial secretary to the Treasury and I was in the chair for the beginning of the L.E.F.T.A. conference on 30 March 1974 at which he (the secretary) and Harold Lever (the chairman) resigned from their positions to take up rather more important jobs in government. I took the opportunity of scolding him severely on this issue. He said that he too had been fighting very hard, but the Inland Revenue were taking the view that it was impossible to bring in a donee-based tax quickly. He asked me to produce a note for him on the subject and I delivered it (at his suggestion) at the House of Commons on Monday, 1 April. It was dated 31 March and I wrote: "What the diligent avoider *has already done* (in order to escape the existing estate duty) is to constitute a network of discretionary and/or accumulating trusts (together with a charitable trust or two to pay his descendants' school fees). I have myself done the former—not the latter! I shall not be satisfied until my beneficiaries are caught. One of the participants at the L.E.F.T.A. meeting of 30 March 1974 said that he personally was professionally engaged in connection with eight trusts in each of which the capital value exceeded £10 million. *These* trusts are what we have to get at and the fatal flaw of the donor-assessed gifts tax is that it will not touch them." I sent him a copy of my Fabian tract reminding him that it contained a draft Bill imposing a donee-assessed tax, and reminding him also that the capital taxation working party had done a lot of work on the difficult problem of applying the tax to settled property. I could not believe that a donee-based tax was as difficult as the Revenue made out. Robert Willis, a recently retired deputy chairman of the Board of Inland Revenue, had admitted that it was administratively feasible at a conference on the Accession Tax called by the Institute of Fiscal Studies on 27 February 1973. All that was needed was a sheet of foolscap for each taxpayer in the class likely to get substantial gifts (numerically a tiny number) recording each gift. Provided the donor was made responsible for collecting the tax at source, there was no problem.

"In addition to the fact that these trusts will escape, another flaw in a donor-assessed gifts tax is that unless you are going to forbid rich people from becoming ordinarily resident abroad (which is unthinkable), they are going to do what they are already doing in increasing numbers—emigrating for a year or two—and then making their gifts to U.K. residents from abroad. Finally it will do nothing to prevent existing taxpayers resident in the U.K. from benefiting from foreign trusts. It is important that an injustice of this sort should not now be *started*."

Holding the views I held about the importance of taxation, I felt passionately on the issue. I would rather the Government did not introduce the tax at all until a donee-based tax was ready. Here was a matter of crucial importance which was being mishandled. One of the troubles was, said John, that Nicholas Kaldor's memoranda on taxation matters always had the Chancellor's eye before his own. It was that man again! Kaldor, indeed, asked me to send him copies of the work I had done on assessing discretionary (and other) trusts to the gifts tax, which I duly did. But it was no real use, because the work was done on the basis that the donee would be assessable to tax. The donor-based tax was also unfair as between individuals: a large family with only one benefactor was hit very hard, whereas a single child with a number of benefactors could receive far too much. But the real charge against it was that anyone who (like me) had made a children's accumulator trust before 1974, escaped C.T.T. entirely. It was a tragedy of bungled opportunity. That I could do nothing about it although I was reasonably close to the two politicians most closely involved, drove me nearly to despair.

Another message was beginning to get home to me: the powerlessness of even the most competent politicians (and I have the highest regard for Denis Healey and John Gilbert) in the face of their officials. I refuse to believe that it was administratively impossible to make the C.T.T. donee based. The trouble was that our precious politicians are just not strong enough to over-rule their officials when the latter get the bit between their teeth.

Another cause close to my heart was the nationalisation of land. After the 1970 election (when I was still working at Transport House) I persuaded Terry Pitt to have me appointed to a land study group reporting to the home policy sub-committee of the N.E.C. on the use and ownership of land. The study group was chaired by John Silkin. I had, I thought, a new idea of how land could be nationalised in a perfectly painless way which, although it would take time, would involve no administrative troubles or gigantic state compensation. As the study group progressed I discovered that the idea had a long history. The germs of it are to be found in the discussions of the Uthwatt Committee in 1942, but the proposal was first aired specifically in *Socialist Commentary* in 1961.

If that land study group was a typical example of how the

Labour Party's policy was formulated in opposition, then it was time the method was altered. A huge group of people was nominated: Members of Parliament, distinguished academics, trades unionists and other outsiders. With a few notable exceptions, no one attended every meeting and consequently most of the time at our later meetings was spent in going over ground that had been previously trodden when the irregular (but none the less voluble for that) attenders were not there. The M.P.s were not only some of the more voluble but also particularly bad attenders because the study group met during sittings of the House of Commons and they had their parliamentary duties to perform.

It soon became apparent that there was a sharp cleavage of opinion between the "whole-hoggers" led by Robert Neild, myself and Joan Maynard, on the one hand; and the chairman, the academics (who had all, it seemed, committed themselves on this issue years and years ago and couldn't possibly change their minds), and most of the trades unionists on the other.

Robert's and my plan was a simple one: contained in our minority report to the home policy sub-committee which we subsequently published as *The Case for Nationalising Land*. Our idea was that on the appointed day, all land in Britain, without exception, should be converted from freehold into ninety-nine-year leasehold at a peppercorn rent on the terms of a statutory lease. The details were quite complicated but the two main evils of the then system of land tenure system were removed. The two main evils were that people were able to make themselves fortunes from decisions of their local planning authority, and that land needed for a public purpose was not always available. In either of these cases, the statutory lease would come to an end, but its owner then had rights to substantial compensation and to the grant of a new lease. No one ever pointed out a technical flaw in our argument. The result of our proposal would be that every landowner would find himself in the correct relationship with the community which was that of landlord and tenant. We left entirely open (on purpose) the question of who or what the local "land management authority" might be except to propose that it should not be confined to politicians. It was really a thoroughly "Right wing" proposal. If 999 years had been substituted for ninety-nine years throughout, no one would have objected. The value of our proposal really rested in its attempt to simplify our time-consuming and inefficient planning laws.

It was the spectre of nationalising the nation's back gardens which made our proposals distasteful to the career politicians. They thought it might offend their owner-occupier constituents who were, by then, alleged to be 52 per cent of the electorate. This self-interested swallowing of the importance of fostering owner-occupation was, to my mind, one of the more distasteful features of Labour thinking. The Labour Party's chief job should have been to look after the interests of the *poor*. That, I would have claimed, was my reason for belonging to it. With very few exceptions, owner-occupiers were not poor.

To cut a long story short, the "whole-hoggers" (Jack Brocklebank, Joan Maynard, Robert Neild, myself and Nicholas Kaldor who, alerted by Robert to the importance of the issue, made one of his rare appearances at the study group in order to vote) were in a small minority. Lest I be accused of waging a personal vendetta against Kaldor, I would like to record that on this issue he was a tower of strength and the only substantial subscriber to the C.N.L. (as we called the campaign for nationalising land) except for myself.

The result of the majority's endeavours (which were endorsed by the N.E.C. and the Conference despite our campaign) was that the Labour Party was saddled with the study group's recommendations. These were included in the manifesto, and are now entombed in the Community Land Act, 1975. It should have been one of my duties at the G.L.C. to try and defend this measure against the attacks of the minority party (as the Conservatives were called). But it was indefensible, and I used thankfully to leave this task in the capable hands of Norman Howard, the chairman of planning.

I have tried to think of a suitable adjective to qualify the

Community Land Act, but I cannot think of anything which is all-embracingly damning enough to fit the bill. It is everything that national legislation should not be: hastily drafted, unclear in its delegation of powers, immensely expensive for the local authorities to sustain at current interest rates, costly in parliamentary time, and productive of a huge bureaucracy. Its only effect when, if ever, property can be profitably developed again, will be to constipate the already troublesomely long planning process. I have never heard of a single convincing argument in its favour. In other words it is a total disaster, which is not surprising in view of the shambles in which it was conceived. I look forward eagerly to its swift demise.

But this is to digress. Our little battle to have the study group's recommendation upset was something of a success from the publicity point of view. Dick Crossman wrote an enthusiastic article of support in *The Times* (19 September 1973) which, although fatal to the acceptance of the argument, gave it publicity. Well over 2,000 copies of the pamphlet were sold, and a reprint is in demand. It is being used in one open university course. We compiled a register of 110 supporters who subscribed at least £1—including eight Members of Parliament. Even Tony Crosland, whose shadow responsibility this was, muttered something to me at the 1973 Conference about possibly having been able to help if only he had known about it earlier.

Frank Allaun (who was one of the majority in the study group) writing about the campaign in *Labour Weekly* on 21 September 1973 called them "the Stutchbury proposals" with the aim (presumably) of discrediting them in the eyes of the Left by associating a City financier's name with them. (Why else should he have so called them?) I nurse a very special contempt for the Tribunites (who are, after all, meant to be the guardians of the Labour Party's conscience on the matter of sticking to a belief in public ownership) on this issue. There were (in addition to the chairman) a number of them on the study group. When the chips were down and they sensed that their seats might be imperilled by this nationalisation proposal, they showed themselves to be without principle. For, either you believe in public ownership, or you do not. If you do, the first (and probably the only) thing you need to nationalise is the land (you can then take any power you need to control any activity carried on on the land by altering the terms of the relevant lease.) If you do not believe in nationalisation, don't pretend to be the guardian of the party's conscience on this issue by fiddling about with proposals to nationalise totally peripheral activities like banking and insurance.

Here was another reconnaissance which ended in disillusion. The whole argument over this land question convinced me that, when the chips were down and its members came face to face with the consequence of their professed faith, I had joined a party which had not the courage of its own convictions.

CHAPTER SEVEN

THE G.L.C.: FIRST IMPRESSIONS

WHEN I had scored my duck in the general secretaryship ballot, and I could see that there was nothing for me to do at Transport House, I had to find something else to do. So I returned to the City and started an insurance company. I also invested a considerable sum of money in a company called "Know-How Instruction Limited". From observing my children growing up, I had become convinced that the teaching medium of the future (particularly in imparting motor skills: i.e. know-how rather than know-that) would be the television screen, when that medium was extended and enriched by a student's ability to show audio-visual cassettes at the time and place of his own choosing.

One of my old pupils in philosophy at Sussex University (where I had taught part-time for two terms when I was managing director of Save and Prosper), Michael Chanan, came forward with a proposal to do a series of six, hour-long documentaries on the revolution in Oxford philosophy which, roughly speaking, had spanned the teaching lifetime of Professor Sir A. J. Ayer, who was to be the "anchorman" of the series. This, although worth while, was a very expensive project for a private citizen to undertake and unlikely to be profitable. It was therefore quite important for me to find some other line of merchandise in the forthcoming audio-visual cassette "break-through" which would be profitable. I consequently gave two contracts, one to Nick Reid and another to Michael Sclater (of both of whose integrity and good taste I was in no doubt), to make a sex film each which was (*a*) instructional, (*b*) funny and (*c*) in which the act of darkness did not *always* achieve that pitch of perfection portrayed in most of the blue movies I had seen. It seemed to me that in this idea that nothing ever goes wrong the young were being given a totally false impression of what often happens in the sexual act. People learn as much from seeing how things should *not* be done as from seeing how they should be done. I invested very much less money in this second venture than in the philosophy series, and I would not mention the matter at all in connection with my political Aeneid, were this episode not to have its repercussions in my political career.

In the early summer of 1972 I was approached by John Keys, who was the general secretary of the Greater London Regional Council of the Labour Party, to assist him in raising funds for the G.L.C. elections in April 1973. I organised a £50-a-plate fund-raising dinner at the Reform Club on Monday, 29 January 1973, at which Shirley Williams was our guest of honour, and which raised over £2,000 for the cause. I also introduced John to a Labour supporter who (on 13 February 1973) in my presence handed over another £1,000 in five-pound notes. "You can count them if you like," said the generous donor defiantly. "I think I will," said the meticulous John. He sat down, licked his finger and finally pronounced them to be all present and correct—which is my sole experience in a varied life of having actually seen someone look a gift horse in the mouth.

I was on the list of approved Labour candidates for the G.L.C. and one day in June 1972 I was telephoned by the secretary of the Acton party and asked if I would like to be considered as their G.L.C. candidate. Beggars can't be choosers; and I duly attended the selection conference held at Ruskin Hall on 12 July 1972. Why was there no local candidate? I asked innocently. Because any local politician who was any use preferred to be on the Ealing Borough Council. There was no G.L.C. housing estate in the constituency and, to be blunt, the people of Acton could not have cared less about the G.L.C. I won that selection conference on the first ballot.

Not much electioneering was possible before Christmas, because the new electoral register was not published, and the whole campaign was uneventful until the *Sunday People* broke the news about the sex fiend the Labour Party had launched into Acton's midst. "THE MILLIONAIRE AND HIS SEX FILM" was the banner headline of Fred Harrison's story on 19 November above a sober enough looking photograph of me. "Mr Oliver Stutchbury is a man of impeccable character . . . but when it comes to informing people on such personal matters as sex, it seems to me that Mr Stutchbury's judgment is sadly lacking. For he has just spent £20,000 to finance a film aimed at educating teenagers on sexual behaviour . . . The film portrays an unmarried couple, Mike and Marion, copulating three times in various positions. . . . 'It's good clean fun for the 13- to 16-year-olds,' he told me. . . . 'Copulation is a skill that has been practised for years and years and years. Nobody would dream of expecting people to learn to ride a bicycle without seeing somebody else do it first . . . the object is to instruct the young on how to do it.' . . . There was some controversy over the title of the film. 'I wanted to call it "How to screw your girl", but this was considered too bawdy.' "

I was duly hauled before a special meeting of the Acton executive and asked to explain my disgraceful conduct. Luckily, a number of the younger members of the Acton party had a sense of humour. Glen Barnham and Ivor Williams had been my guests at a party to launch the film and they were able to testify that it was not obscene. I confined my defence of myself to saying that there was nothing I was in the least ashamed of (except that I had spoken so freely to Fred Harrison) and I would do the same again if I were faced with the decision of whether or not to finance the film once more.

And that would have been that, but not quite. I was recounting my experiences before the executive to Nigel Spearing, the M.P. for Acton, at dinner in the House of Commons to which he and his wife had kindly invited Helen and me early in the New Year, when I discovered to my surprise that he knew nothing about this episode. The next day he rang up to say (very politely and gently) that he had decided to dissociate himself as far as he reasonably could from my candidature, and would not be campaigning for me in the election. And he was as good as his word. Whether or not it made any difference to the result I do not know. I certainly heard that Tory canvassers were doing their best during the campaign to make known my turpitude to the electorate, but I can't believe it interested the electors.

Most of the electioneering was done on Sundays. On the last Sunday before polling day I dragged up to London sixteen protesting but loyal members of the Stutchbury family to help in the campaign. The effort was of no avail. The count of all three Ealing constituencies was held in the Town Hall at Ealing on 12 April. The Acton result was the last to be announced. David Mason had won Ealing North. Yvonne Sieve had won Ealing Southall. The figures for Ealing Acton were:

Electorate 57,280

J. C. Dobson (C)	10,576
O. P. Stutchbury (L)	9,665
N. J. Reed (Lib)	2,616
H. R. Tank (Comm)	303
Maj.	911

Labour had won control of the G.L.C. but, to my bitter disappointment, Acton had not swung sufficiently. However, at the first meeting of the Labour Group, it was agreed that I should be one of the seven aldermen they were entitled to co-opt to the Council and at the Council meeting on Friday, 4 May 1973, I was duly elected a member of the G.L.C. (restricted only in my ability to vote in the election of other aldermen—otherwise having the same powers, duties and rights as an elected councillor). I am clear that the only reason I attained this eminence was the financial assistance I had been able to give the party and John Keys was repaying me in the best coin at his disposal. So, in the end, I bought my way into politics. I am extremely glad that he did what he did, and am grateful to the Labour Group for giving me the insight into government which my time on the G.L.C. afforded me.

Owing to the malevolence of the late Peggy Middleton, I was one of the handful of Labour members who got no job at all in the first year of Sir Reg Goodwin's administration. Peggy was a picturesque and influential figure at County Hall; and, by reputation, someone who could have great charm and was a magnificent hostess. She was appointed chairman of the Finance Board and (without ever having met me) refused to have me as her vice-chairman. I was never quite clear what she had against me and I had high hopes (before she died suddenly in the recess in 1974) that I would eventually overcome her hostility. In the end it did not matter, because the fact is, illustrating the curiously random way in which fate operates in a politician's career, *not* getting the vice-chairmanship of the Finance Board turned out to be a stroke of the greatest good fortune to me.

I find it difficult to describe my initial bewilderment with the G.L.C. First, there was the building itself. The principal floor was constructed in such a way that the rooms could not be numbered in sequence. So new members found themselves (to the great satisfaction of the old lags) making for the wrong corners of the huge building, hopelessly lost and late for their first meetings. It is to be noted that the official *Members' Guide* (January 1976 edition) contains no plan of the principal floor, which would be its most informative ingredient, so I can only surmise that the officers, too, were pleased to see new members getting lost.

Next, there was the relationship with the staff. As I wrote in the G.L.C. house magazine *London Town* in December 1973, it was not so much that the relationship between the staff and elected members was *bad*, as that the relationship was non-existent. The Council's staff felt remote from the Council but (as a new member of the Council) I felt, not remote from the staff, but on a different planet altogether. I had never experienced anything like it before: in the army, at university or in any of the institutions with which I was used to deal.

The system by which nothing was seen by the elected members until it had been through all the proper channels and had been blessed by one of the chief officers ensured that elected members had no hand in any matter until it became a matter of policy and could not be altered. There was little or no way in which we could alter the course of events at all except by throwing things out, and by the time that we were asked to take the final decision so much preparatory work had been done that it usually seemed to be less expensive to finish the work off than to cancel it. I could for the first two years of my career at County Hall find no way in which anyone could stick a sharp object into the hippopotamus's hide and make the monumental animal budge an inch in any direction or even notice any attempt to get it to respond.

My first initiative was ill-judged. I put down a motion at the Labour Group saying that since the success or otherwise of our administration would be exclusively determined by the amount of money we were able to extract from central government, the chief officers should be instructed as a matter of urgency to prepare plans of ways in which we could twist central government's arm if our demands were not met: like arranging for the fire brigade to foul up traffic in Parliament Square at the Opening of Parliament, or closing Westminster Underground Station, or refusing to collect refuse from Downing Street, Whitehall or the Palace of Westminster. The old guard was not amused. Among other things, it showed my deplorable ignorance: refuse *collection* was a matter for the boroughs, our role being limited to refuse *disposal*.

Against Peggy Middleton's and the officers' initial hostility and resentment (a letter from the Comptroller of Financial Services to the chairman of the Finance Board dated 17 July 1973 which Peggy sent on to me with a hand-written scrawl: "Dear Mr Stutchbury, I think the above answers your questions . . . (squiggle, squiggle) . . . Peggy Middleton", ended: "You will, of course, recognise at once that the expressing of unfounded suspicions and allegations can be, at best, extremely damaging to the interests of the G.L.C."), I uncovered what seemed to me to be an archaic and unsatisfactory way of insuring the Council's very substantial properties. This was eventually changed for the better. Sniping from the side-lines could sometimes produce a tiny result.

Undeterred by Peggy's indifference to my opinions, I used to send her letters of advice. I wrote her a long letter from Blackpool (dated 30 September 1973) on an officer's paper called "The Provision of Capital Finance" in which I wrote that I detected a fundamental misunderstanding about long-term trends in interest rates. "They may decline *marginally* over the next few months—but I believe that in the future we can expect them to fluctuate between 12 per cent and 15 per cent; so that 12 per cent will be seen in the future to be historically at the low end of the scale." I sent a copy of this letter to the Leader's private office, and when I proved to be more right in my guess than the officers, my stock began to rise in that all-important location.

I must also confess to a letter I wrote to the Chief Whip on 12 October 1973 because it shows that, at that time, I was still possessed of the mistaken idea that the G.L.C. could achieve something useful. I was protesting at a decision to take office accommodation for the architect's department in Regent Street at £8 per square foot per annum. What disturbed me was the complete absence of any indication of forward planning for what I hoped would be a mammoth increase in the Council's staff over the next ten years. As a Socialist I believed in the expansion of public sector services, but there was no possible justification for housing the bureaucracy in the most expensive parts of London. We should be planning a new County Hall at (say) Thamesmead. It should be an office complex to house twice (or three times) the number of people who currently worked at County Hall. I would like, too, to put on record that there was one really farsighted Labour G.L.C. member, Andrew McIntosh, who told me I was talking rot and that he wouldn't be satisfied until the sprawl of G.L.C. bureaucracy was thinned out sufficiently so that it could once again fit into County Hall.

At the beginning of 1974 there was the general election fought on the issue of Mr Heath's confrontation with the miners. As a law and order man, I was in a serious fix. On 9 February, *The*

Times published a letter from me to which I have never had any answer. "Some of us in the Labour Party believe that the primary task of the next Labour government is to legislate against the unacceptable inequalities in the distribution of wealth in this country. This will mean imposing a progressive Accessions Tax and a Wealth Tax. I have no doubt that these measures will not be popular among the rich, and were, say, the Country Landowners' Association to hold a secret ballot among its members it would have no difficulty in securing an 80 per cent majority for a proposal to authorise its executive to organise a taxpayers' strike against these measures. Although such a strike would not bring the country to its knees, it could render the measures largely ineffective. Would someone more skilled in this kind of dialectic than I am please explain how, in these circumstances, one could distinguish between the action of the C.L.A. and the action of the N.U.M. in its current strike? If one cannot distinguish between the two, and one hopes a future Labour Government accepts the responsibility outlined in my first paragraph, is not the Labour Party, by espousing the N.U.M.'s cause, delivering a valuable hostage to fortune?" Oddly enough, this letter had no political repercussions on me—perhaps because so few Labour supporters read *The Times*. I cannot pretend it was other than the act of a coward, but on Friday, 15 February I left on Flight No. TW771 bound for Denver, Colorado, and did not show my face in England again until the day before the election. I did not contemplate resigning from the Labour Party because I was still possessed of this bug that a gifts tax must be introduced and I couldn't see that the Tories were likely to do it. (And when the Labour Party did, they bungled it.)

In May 1974, Dr David Pitt, the vice-chairman of the Policy and Resources Committee, was elevated to the chairmanship of the Council in what was a brilliant appointment by the Leader and his advisers. This left a vacancy in a key office, because the chairman of Policy and Resources was Illtyd Harrington, the colourful Deputy Leader, who rightly delegated much of the detailed work of his committee to his second-in-command.

I do not know by what stroke of luck the Leader's Advisory Committee selected me for the job. I have a sneaking feeling (for which I have no evidence) that I was Illtyd's choice because he could think of no appointment which would annoy Peggy Middleton more. Her Finance Board reported to Policy and Resources, and the mutual antipathy of Illtyd and Peggy was one of the more amusing sideshows of the Second Division League politics in which we played our parts. Anyway, I got the job and my two and a half years as vice-chairman of Policy and Resources will (I imagine on present evidence) be the highest place in politics I shall ever climb to.

I enjoyed every minute of it; not least because I shared a room with Illtyd, who was a most amusing and entertaining companion, unfailing in his courtesy, charm and consideration for his room-mate, and the most formidable political orator in our G.L.C. team. I immensely enjoyed the social life surrounding the G.L.C.—the bar and members' refreshment room. I simply loved the politics: ganging up with X, Y and Z to defeat W's motion to Group; forming a little cabal to see that some chairman did not get his way over something or other. The work was not over-intensive as it seemed to be in the First Division League (politics over the river at Westminster)—indeed, if the truth were known, there was not really enough to do (and the more indigent members had to use their ingenuity to get themselves given "approved duties" which attracted some sort of payment)—but there seemed to me to be just the right amount to do. As I'd always suspected, I just loved the life.

In the event, I had only one serious brush with Peggy and that was over a matter which still troubles my conscience. It will be recalled that in the 1974 general election, Harold Wilson was returned with no overall majority in the House of Commons. There was a general expectation that there would be another election in the autumn, and (as good Labour Party men) it was our duty to do all we could to shore up the Government in the meanwhile. But one can take party loyalty too far.

Interest rates were shooting up. Whereas the Council had been able to offer loans to borrowers on its house purchase scheme at 11 per cent, it became clear that, if there was not to be a subsidy from the ratepayer, the G.L.C. would have to put up the rate of interest to 13 per cent. This would have appeared to be in breach of the Government's counter-inflation policy and the Leader, Peggy Middleton and myself (with officers) trooped dutifully across Westminster Bridge to argue this out with the Ministers (one of whom, in my view, was too dim to see the point of principle involved). We were adamant (as were our officers) that we ought not to ask ratepayers to pay this subsidy. If central government wanted to pay it, that was another matter. The Leader was particularly involved because he had originally introduced the scheme to the Council, many years previously, on the basis that it would cost the ratepayers nothing. In our final interview with the Secretary of State, he came without his civil servants, and we went without our officers. He then pleaded with us to hold the rate until after the projected autumn election, not because it was the right thing to do, but because the right thing to do would be detrimental to the party's prospects in the election. As we came back over Westminster Bridge, I thought the Leader had made up his mind to stand firm. But he, of course, had to weigh what was right against what was in the best interests of London.

The meeting with the Secretary of State was on Friday, 5 July and afterwards I went to the country for the week-end. On my return to County Hall on Tuesday I was surprised and disturbed to discover that the Leader had made a decision to leave the rate of interest on the home loans scheme where it was. I wrote a long memorandum to the Finance Board Group which met on 11 July. "I respectfully disagree with the Leader's decision . . . the principal reason is set out thus in the Leader's letter to Mr Crosland of 11 June: 'What you are asking us to do is to subsidise around 700 named house-purchasers per month, chosen because they happen to be buying a house in the month in question (and not very poor people at that) for the duration of their loans or until interest rates fall below 11 per cent (whichever is the shorter) *at the expense* of other claims on the rates.' . . . These strong reasons are not denied: so one must examine the strength of the opposing arguments which are: '(*a*) I, as Secretary of State, have done a lot for London ratepayers by altering the basis of the R.S.G. in favour of the urban authorities; (*b*) for the largest authority in the country to put up interest rates on its home loans scheme to what is effectively 13 per cent would be crucially damaging to the Government's anti-inflationary policy; (*c*) I grant the strength of all your arguments but ask you for the sake of the Labour Government and good relations between us, to keep the interest rate at 11 per cent until after the next election but I am afraid I cannot give you any central government help in doing so.' Has the Secretary of State done a lot for London ratepayers? Even after the Secretary of State's intervention, London—as a whole—receives only some 40 per cent of expenditure by way of grant as against 58 per cent in the rest of the country (cf. the Comptroller's R.S.G. Paper of 24 April 1974). . . . Would it be crucially damaging to the Government's anti-inflationary policy if the rate went up to 13 per cent? Not, in my submission, if we confine applicants to those who wish to make use of the low start/option mortgage scheme. Such applicants pay no more than 9 per cent. The final reason is the worst sort of political blackmail. . . ." There was a bad attendance at the Labour Finance Group meeting and Peggy won with her chairman's casting vote. Then I let the matter drop.

I could (and possibly should) have resigned, and brought the whole thing out into the open. But what good would it have done? I was just beginning to savour the taste of (as I thought) a little political power. If I resigned, it would have been forgotten in a week; and my chances of further political promotion would have been gone for ever. But I felt myself tainted. I was caught up in something which, in the business world, I would have called *crooked* (and would never have agreed to for motives of self-preservation). But, or so I am told, if one is to survive in that dirty world of politics, one has to accept the need to do things which are not strictly honest. That is the argument, but I am not convinced.

Despite this rebellion (or it may have been because of it) I was made chairman of a special committee of the Council which gave evidence to the Layfield Committee of Enquiry into local government finance. I began to learn about the Rate Support Grant which is the principal source of local government finance in the United Kingdom. In 1976, the amount transferred from central government to the local authorities came to £6,852 million and I must go into the R.S.G. in some detail because I finally became convinced that the way the R.S.G. operated was a complete shambles and, like a clutch which slips in a car, was leading to a breakdown in the machinery of government in Great Britain.

The Rate Support Grant is composed of three elements: the "needs" element, the "resources" element, and the "domestic" element. There are different ways of calculating the needs element for different parts of the country, but an indication of the complications involved can be given by listing the ten factors which were taken into account (and the amount of money received therefor) in calculating the *needs* element for the Outer London Boroughs in the seventh period 1976/77:

£1.36	×	Population at 30.6.75
£5.81	×	
£0.255	×	1,000 population of the area (30.6.75) × decline in population between 30.6.70 and 30.6.75.
£1,346.30	×	Number of new permanent dwellings (public and private sectors) started in the area during period 1.4.75 to 31.3.76.
£77.21	×	Number of Education units (January 1976) in excess of 223 per 1,000 population (30.6.75).
£222.80	×	Number of persons of pensionable age living alone (1971 Census Data) in excess of 17 per 1,000 population (30.6.75).
£56.57	×	Number of persons in permanent buildings with a density of occupation greater than 1½ persons

per room (1971 Census Data) in excess of 10 per 1,000 population (30.6.75).

£1,587.30 × Number of children in care (31.3.74) in excess of 67 per 100,000 population (30.6.75). (The number of children in care for each area shall be the number notified to the Secretary of State by the Greater London Council for R.S.G. purposes.)

£4.35 × Number of day time population (1971 Census Data) in excess of 819 per 1,000 population (30.6.75). The daytime population shall be ascertained by taking aggregate number of persons resident in area, and number of persons working but not resident in area (1971 Census Data) and deducting number of persons resident in but working outside area (1971 Census Data).

£1.922 × 1,000 population (30.6.75) × increase in population between 30.6.70 to 30.6.75.

£98.08% × 1975–76 needs element entitlement (Pre Increase Order 1975).

As Mervyn Scourgie, one of the Conservative members of the G.L.C., remarked, the only factor of any consequence (and just as relevant) *not* taken into account was the menstrual cycle of the Secretary of State's wife. There was a passage in Annex 2 of the Fourth Report of the Grants Working Party which particularly took my fancy: "Principal Components Analysis produces from a set of *correlated* variables a set of *uncorrelated* variables. Complete understanding of this procedure is not possible without knowledge of advanced mathematics. This note provides a simplified description of the basic principles involved . . ." I read on but could make neither head nor tail of the simplified description.

I wish I could give an adequate description of the aura of mystery, majesty and importance which attended the joint meetings of the A.M.A., A.C.C. and A.D.C., when the local authority bigwigs congregated to be told the attitude that the Department was taking in the R.S.G. negotiations, and what their response should be. One hundred or so of the senior figures in local government (the Leader, the Director-General and the Comptroller of Financial Services would think it necessary to attend, if they could) from England and Wales would congregate to receive the officials' report on what line to take. But the outcome was known to be a completely *random* decision. The emperor had no clothes at all. I became increasingly incensed with the whole process because it gave a specious appearance of scientific respectability to a decision which ended by being totally arbitrary.

The Layfield Report (Cmnd. 6453) has now spelt out in words of one syllable just how haphazard the R.S.G. negotiations are. As far as London was concerned (which was my interest) we would have had no particular quarrel with the amount of money which came our way if we were treated like other authorities. But our share was diminished by a totally arbitrary amount called "clawback". This piece of daylight robbery was made politically possible only by the complete ignorance of far too many of London's ninety-two Members of Parliament of the crucial effect of the R.S.G. decision. It was *by far* the most important thing which happened each year in internal public administration in this country, but most politicians could not be bothered with it. As far as the local authorities (other than the A.M.A.) were concerned, they were delighted with "clawback" because less for London meant more for them. Because they tended to equate London with central government (which they despised with all the intensity of the Scottish and Welsh Nationalists) they were perfectly happy with anything unpleasant which happened to London.

The unfairly diminished proportion of the total which went to London was so inequitably divided between the individual London boroughs by the formula, that the individual boroughs then got together at a private tea-party at which they decided *voluntarily* how the R.S.G. was to be fairly redistributed between them. (What is one to make of a formula which, when fed with the effect of London weighting on the local authorities salary bill, comes out with a result that distributes most of the cash increase to authorities outside London—which, by definition, do not pay London weighting?) This private tea-party at which the London rate equalisation scheme (as it is called) was achieved voluntarily, was arranged by an unpublicised and inconspicuous organisation called the London Boroughs Association, chaired by Sir Lou Sherman, who was, in my opinion, London's most effective politician. All I wish to do at this point in my journey is to point to it as a highly effective and economical political institution. It could well prove to be the sort of top tier regional authority we ought to have in England and Wales.

The reason I have likened the R.S.G. to a slipping clutch in the machinery of government is this. The most important fact in all local authority decision-taking should be: how much is this going to cost? How much it is going to cost depends as to two-thirds of the expenditure on the grant from central government. One needs years of experience to understand the implications of the grant, and over quite a range of its activities a local authority hasn't any idea what the grant will be. The result is that very many crucial decisions are taken in the dark as far as the most important fact which should be taken into account is concerned.

The second fact about local government which I learnt the hard way through personal experience was its total dependence in practice on central government decision (or more often, central government indecision so that local authorities have to wait). The *received* view of what happens is that within certain limits, the local authorities can spend how they choose what they raise in rates and get in grant. The G.L.C. is responsible for strategic planning, housing, transport, health and safety in the capital; the boroughs are responsible for local planning, housing and personal social services; and the responsibility for education is split between the Inner London Education Authority and the outer boroughs. But within these limits the local authorities can allocate the money as they like.

This is not the way it works in practice. When the Labour Party took control of the G.L.C. in 1973, we were pledged, among other things, to peg London Transport fares and to support a big increase in house acquisition in the public sector. Whether this was the right programme to have adopted in view of the massive dose of inflation to which we were all to be subjected is another matter. There was no doubt that the Labour Party was pledged to it; and it was certainly not the wish of the elected members that these policies were abandoned. It was the direct result of the D.O.E. Circular 171/1974, coupled with a nod which was as threatening as a wink from the Treasury, through the Bank of England, that if the G.L.C. were stupid enough to do what the Minister of Housing was even then upbraiding us for *not* doing (i.e. continuing with our original house-building programme), we would have to borrow money from the Public Works Loans Board at 2 per cent per annum above the quota rate.

My own response to 171/1974 was contained in a memorandum dated 18 March 1975 which I circulated to the Leader's Budget Advisory Group. "It is not a bad thing that the full implications of central government policy should have hit the G.L.C. almost exactly half way through Labour's current term of office because it gives the majority party time to make a radical change of course before the next G.L.C. elections in 1977. The Labour Group must realise that central government policy: (*a*) makes a *public* sector solution to London's housing problems totally unrealistic; (*b*) forces the G.L.C. to run London Transport on capitalist lines and renders the majority party's declared transport policy incapable of implementation; and (*c*) ensures that unless central government can be persuaded to make the G.L.C. an exception, the G.L.C. will continue to be an extremely bad landlord. The *first* decision for the Group is whether or not it is prepared to be the agent of central government for policies which are not socialist. It is for serious consideration whether the Labour Group should not consider putting Mr Cutler and his boys in the position of being the majority party, even if for only a limited period of time (say three months)." Of course the Leader's Budget Advisory Group thought that this course was unthinkable. I, personally, continue to think it would have been the most honest thing to do.

I went on: "If it is the majority view that this move is unthinkable, then a *radical* change of direction must be made in the G.L.C.'s capital spending. . . . The Government must be told that a public sector solution to London's housing problems is impossible within the present local authority strait-jacket, and central government must have the courage to foster the private sector with tax concessions to landlords, and tax concessions to *all* tenants (public and private sector). If the private sector is thus encouraged the G.L.C.: (1) can afford to abandon all its housing construction and assistance outside the G.L.C. area; (2) can abandon its programme of making loans to housing associations and home loans; (3) should acquire no more sites until Thamesmead is fully developed; (4) should abandon its programme of acquiring existing dwellings and dwellings under construction; and (5) should look very carefully again at the £11 million budgetted for 'strategic planning' in 1975–6. Adoption of any part of the above policy will involve a major administrative upheaval at County Hall and this is unreservedly to be welcomed. The administrative (and other) inefficiency at County Hall is giving public sector activity a very bad name. It must be a major goal to improve before 1977 the G.L.C.'s appalling administrative image." Not surprisingly I wasn't able to get my colleagues to endorse these recommendations. They had known these Government circulars before, and policy had changed too often for them to be over-concerned.

The belief that the private sector in rented accommodation should be resuscitated was one I had held for a long time. A letter of mine about it was published in *The Times* on 25 September 1971. When Anthony Crosland published his Herbert Morrison memorial lecture *Towards a Labour Housing Policy* (Fabian Tract 410), we had him to lunch at Save and Prosper (from which I then still derived my livelihood) on 29

November 1971. Denis Pilcher (a colleague on the board) and I tried to convince him of the need for the Labour Party to do something on these lines, if there were to be any help for the *really* poor (far too many of whom eventually found their way into the private rented sector). I was never able to get Crosland to move an inch on this.

I remain convinced that similar tax advantages to the tenants of rented accommodation (i.e. the deduction of rent from gross income for tax purposes) as are available to owner-occupier mortgagors, and similar capital allowances to people who provide private sector rented accommodation as are available for industrial investment, together with the gradual dismantling of rent controls, is the only sensible way of solving London's housing problems. Far too much of the public sector activity in this area is grossly inefficient for it ever to be able to do the job alone; and owner-occupation is not a solution for the poor.

CHAPTER EIGHT

HOUGHTON AND THE NEED OF A NEW PARTY

THE essence of politics, we are always told, is timing. Lurking at the back of my political mind all this time was the conviction that the Labour Party organisation would soon go bust. At that moment there would be a possibility of opening up the membership so that it was not so dismayingly class-fixated and tied to the unions' apron-strings as it was and would grow into the left-centre party that so many of my non-political friends would be happy to support, although at that time they felt that it was wrong to vote Labour. But I should have foreseen that the System would have an answer to that one.

For some reason I missed the announcement in the House of Commons on 8 May 1975 that a committee under Lord Houghton's chairmanship had been established to consider the question of financial aid to political parties. When, afterwards, I spotted a report in *The Times* that the N.E.C. had given evidence to the committee in favour of state aid, I could see that one of my most cherished dreams was about to be nipped in the bud. The thought of the poor old taxpayer being asked to subsidise Transport House or Conservative Central Office was a good deal more than I could stand without protest.

I lost no time in registering an objection with a letter to *The Times*, and wrote to Lord Houghton on 14 July offering to give oral evidence but adding: "In my considered opinion there would be little difficulty in the Labour Party raising the £3 million annually needed to run its machine satisfactorily, if only it would take minimal steps to reorganise its organisation in the country. How this should be done is set out in my contribution to Fabian Tract 407, two copies of which I enclose. There is no particular need for you to plough through my suggestions. The point is that I could not even get them *considered* by the organisation sub-committee of the N.E.C. It just does not suit the national agent's department to change the existing shambles. Moreover, in the country at large, far too many Constituency Labour Parties (particularly in safe Labour seats) are controlled by people whom it does not suit to have to change their ways to attract a larger membership. In this situation it would be quite wrong for the state to perpetuate the existing undesirable set-up by subsidising it. It would be much better for the Labour Party to go bust, and be forced to recast its machinery on more democratic lines."

I gave evidence to the committee on 4 August. It turned out to be a replay of the old arguments I used to have with Reg Underhill at Transport House. Reg Underhill was (as, no doubt, was to be expected) a member of the committee, together with another typical female Labour Party organisation stalwart. The composition of the committee had been carefully selected for political balance. But there was no representative of the overwhelming majority of the country who think that politics is a distracting waste of time, money and energy, and that the less we have of it, the better we would all be served.

I did not let the matter rest with my evidence to Houghton. I made (I thought) one of my more effective speeches in Council on the topic on 25 November 1975—committing myself to looking upon the matter as an issue of principle which would cause me to resign from the Labour Party if it became law under a Labour Government. Debates in Council were something of a puzzle—the puzzle being whether to speak or not. When the Whips were on, there was no doubt that one was just wasting time by speaking. But on this occasion the Whips were off, and the Council passed, by a substantial majority, a motion condemning the extension of the practice of giving money to the existing party machines.

But the wise people like my colleague Stanley Mayne who had known the System for a long time, insisted that, although regrettable, state subsidies for the political parties were inevitable. It seemed to me *incredible* that any right-minded person would not see where we were being led. But, I had to remind myself, things that had seemed to me incredible in the past, like the appointment of Ron Hayward as general secretary of the Labour Party, had indeed come to pass. On 1 March 1976, David Wood wrote an authoritative article in *The Times* saying that it was going to happen and that he, for one, doubted if any matter of democratic principle were involved.

I summoned up all my confused but violent thoughts about the topic and wrote an article, some of which was published in *The Times* on 21 March 1976. The real danger in the proposals I argued was the monstrous increase in political patronage that this would confer on the leaders of the existing political parties—not just the Prime Minister of the day, but the opposition parties too. When in office he would (and already did) propose members of the opposition parties for honours and jobs at the behest of their leaders in the confident expectation of getting reciprocity when he was out of office. This was part of the System. We would end up with what was, in effect, a one-party state and there would be no way of sacking the government which (as Lord Goodman had recently pointed out) was the true hallmark of a democracy.

I also sounded off my, by now well-worn, diatribe about the uselessness of the political party machines. This particular argument of mine did not exactly endear me to my old friend John Keys, the general secretary of the London Labour Party and his colleagues at Herbert Morrison House. "Are you trying to tell us," said John plaintively but appositely, "that we are wasting our lives?" My honest answer should have been, yes they were wasting their lives as I had wasted four years of my life when I first left the City. "The question," I wrote, "which needs to be examined is whether the existence of the party machines is necessary to the preservation of democracy. The received answer is that the machines have four functions without which democracy cannot survive: selecting candidates, undertaking research, formulating policy, and getting candidates elected.

"Clearly the selection of candidates is essential to democracy, but do the party political machines do it well? My answer is that they do not. I do not see how anyone in the Labour Party can be happy about a selection process which produces the situation in Newham North-East where a Cabinet minister has been refused reselection because a handful of the people who vote for him dislike his politics. Nor do I think that the Conservative Party selection process has thrown up an outstandingly able front bench in the House of Commons. I am inclined to think that almost anything (perhaps primary elections) would be better than the present system.

"What about the need to do research? That is already being done (without state subsidy) in overwhelming quantity by the Acton Society, the Fabian Society, P.E.P., the Institute of Economic Affairs, the individual trades unions, journalists of every political complexion, and academics. Why do we need a state subsidy to do more research?

"It is important for democracy that political parties should have policies, but it is less obvious that we need machines to formulate policies. What on earth are the front benches of the House of Commons for? The dignity of Parliament is not enhanced if policy is formulated somewhere else.

"The function of getting candidates elected is a convenience to the successful candidate but not essential to democracy. Since there are always fewer successful than unsuccessful candidates in elections, it follows that the machines perform this function rather poorly (they could not do otherwise).

"I conclude that the party political machines are not essential to democracy and therefore do not deserve subsidy."

What was really disturbing me was a gradual loss of hope that anything could be done about the deplorable way in which Great Britain was governed. I was invited to address the political society at my old school (Radley) on 12 October 1975 and chose as my subject "The Radical Predicament". I identified three public scandals which could only be solved by root and branch reforms: (1) the conditions in our prisons; (2) that we manufacture and sell at a profit to savages and barbarians, weapons which they can and do use to kill and maim one another; and (3) that there were something like 100,000 homeless family units in the U.K. but many more empty homes than this, and we didn't seem able to marry the two. To get something done about these scandals one had to become a career politician: a breed that was generally despised. The paradigm of the successful politician was a man who was then prominent in public life, of whom it was generally agreed that, first he had no principles except that his own interest must be served first; second, that he had no loyalties to anyone except his ex-mistress; and third, that he had no beliefs of any kind except in himself. How had he come to be so successful?

The key decision-making bodies in British politics, I argued, were not the individual politicians themselves, not the political parties, not the electorate, but the party groups in the various tiers of government. It was the party groups in Parliament which had elected to their exalted positions the various persons who then led us. I could only speak with assurance about the Labour Group on the G.L.C., but I had many close friends and colleagues in the House of Commons who assured me that, *mutatis mutandis*, it was the same there. Council debates in the G.L.C. were a formality. Decisions were taken at Group meetings; it was there that one had to make one's name. It was there that one could not afford to have radical views or propose radical solutions.

Why not? When a member of the Group came to a collective decision on any matter, he was primarily consulting his own self-interest. He took two things into account: first, would this decision advance his career?—this very often transformed itself into the converse: would this decision dish his good friend and colleague so-and-so (who happened to be his chief rival for some post or office he coveted); and secondly, would this decision offend anyone in his constituency party? It was this second factor which made the constituency parties so frightfully important. Richard Crossman had confirmed this in his *Diaries* (Vol. I,

Hamish Hamilton and Jonathan Cape, 1975, p. 416): "What a book one could write about the influence the constituency exerts on the M.P. The luck of my being chosen in 1937 has kept me in Parliament with a huge cast-iron majority and with a particular kind of Party behind me which has deeply influenced (my) thinking, keeping me much more to the Left than I would by nature have been."

It was, incidentally, the first factor which provided the explanation of why we had such lousy leaders. Your Groups were composed exclusively of ambitious politicians, and if someone could not get himself elected as leader, he would choose the candidate over whom he thought he could exert most influence. This mixture was a sure way for getting the most indecisive and irresolute man or woman around.

In the sequel to the passage just quoted Crossman goes on to confess that he is aware of a decline in his Constituency Labour Party. This was my theme in my *Times* article. "The fact is that the activists in the main parties today are extremists—not political extremists, but extremists in another sense. Since the tasks the political machines are called upon to perform are for the most part extremely boring—canvassing, attending party conferences, listening to politicians making speeches—only people with extremely high boredom thresholds volunteer for the task. Not surprisingly the number is constantly dwindling, and the young have better things to do.

"These are the 'activists' to whom our politicians proudly refer as the 'grass-roots'. When politicans visit their constituencies, these are the people they meet. At Westminster they talk to one another. Any other personal contacts they make will be a statistically insignificant sample of the population. Since they receive a wholly unrepresentative view of what their electorate is thinking from the activists, it is no wonder that there are complaints that they are not 'in touch' with ordinary people."

(My remarks about the activists did not, alas, go unread in the Islington Central Constituency Labour Party where I was shortlisted for the G.L.C. candidacy on Dame Evelyn Denington's retirement. I was trying to get a Labour candidacy because the office of alderman was being abolished. Did this mean that I thought they were all morons? someone asked, having read out the offending passage to the selection conference. It was not *quite* what I meant, but I hadn't a carefully prepared answer. I got one vote out of thirty-eight and was eliminated on the first ballot.)

The core of the radical predicament, I told my audience of Radleians, was the impossibility of getting a party group to consider anything radical because it was bound to upset some determined section of activists. On prisons, the politician would offend the trades unions and every member of the group who wanted to spend money on other personal social services. Prisoners have no friends among the activists. On exporting arms, he would offend the trades unions and every serviceman, ex-serviceman, and capitalist making profits, the Foreign Office, the Bank of England (Exchange Control), and the U.S. State Department. The people likely to be maimed or killed would have no friends. On housing his solutions would be likely to offend all local authority and other statutory tenants (in one party) and owner-occupiers too if his solutions included being beastly to building society tax concessions. My conclusion was that given the existing structure of the party machines no politician could ever muster a majority of his group in support of radical measures.

I was enchanted with the title of, and the analysis contained in, a book published at about this time called *95 Per Cent is Crap: A plain man's guide to British Politics* (Libertarian Books Ltd, 1975). It was written by an actuary called Terry Arthur who had collected excerpts of leading politicians' speeches quoted in the *Guardian* over a two-year period and analysed them for content, which he found wanting.

I even toyed with the idea of launching a Crusade Against Political Parties or a Campaign Against Professional Politicians (I was never quite sure which it should be) with the slogan *CAPP against CRAP* in an effort to alert the public to the dangers of the

CHAPTER NINE

THE G.L.C.: MY FINAL PHASE

IF there is a theme running through this book it is my impression of the short-sighted incompetence of the overwhelming majority of my fellow politicians, coupled with disgust at their preoccupation with their own self-interest. I do not exonerate them from the charge of consulting their own self-interest, but in this respect they are no different from all other human beings, including myself. Where I have changed my view recently, in what is an all-embracing conversion, is that I no longer question the competence of the bulk of politicians. I have come to believe that no politician or party or combination of politicians or parties (such as a national coalition) can possibly do anything about our system of government and we are accelerating towards its collapse.

It is by no means a novel viewpoint. I had been aware for some years of the work of James Robertson, but it was not until I read an article about him in a national newspaper over the Christmas holidays in 1975 that I realised that I was just beginning to see very dimly what he had been preaching for some years. He has recently restated his theme in *Power, Money and Sex* (Marion Boyars, 1976). Robertson put me in touch with Peter Cadogan, another prophet with a very similar message, who has produced a privately printed pamphlet, *Direct Democracy,* which bears reading again and again for the insight it brings to our present predicament.

My way of putting their message would be this. In Great Britain today, the individual citizen is being crippled by overmighty government. The outstanding political issue is not a difference between the parties, but between the people themselves and the "established institutions" by which they are governed. Among these institutions must be included:

Parliament itself established at Westminster, the G.L.C., the civil service, the trades unions, the members of the C.B.I. and the other large public and private monopolies (e.g. the area gas boards and the clearing banks) which supply people with very many of the goods and services they cannot do without.

These established institutions are: (*a*) out of anyone's control; (*b*) growing inexorably in size; and (*c*) strangling the national economy and the taxpayer as they steadily absorb an increasing proportion of the national wealth while achieving, on any reckoning, no more than they have achieved in the past.

So far from helping to find a solution to this problem, the present party political structure renders it incapable of solution. The method of selection, training and advancement of career politicians ensures that we will always be governed by people who wish to perpetuate the system as it is. Their ambition is one day to be the cocks strutting round importantly but impotently on the top of the dung-heap, in place of the people who are there now. We have no machinery at hand to upset the System. We are thus rapidly becoming a corporate state with a growing superstructure of "government" which is sending us headlong along the road to national bankruptcy.

If this, at first, seemed to me to be an extreme view I was continually confirmed in it as I tried to exercise such power as I had at the G.L.C. I will give three instances of this from my last months at County Hall, but they can be buttressed by many more examples and I do not want these three instances to be cited as my only reasons for holding the views I now hold. Each time I crossed Westminster Bridge on a high-level delegation to Whitehall I was struck by the rigidity of the ceremonial. It was a ritual to no discernible end. We would be ushered into a room with name boards in front of each place. Shortly afterwards the Secretary of State, Minister (or whoever) would arrive surrounded by a covey of civil servants. The politicians would make chortling noises and gestures to one another, and then everyone would sit down.

The Secretary of State/Minister would then say a few words of welcome, mentioning how very glad he was to have the opportunity of speaking to us *personally* on this very important/difficult/troublesome problem. Then depending on who had initiated the meeting, the head of the G.L.C. or Whitehall delegation would speak to a brief for at least five minutes. The brief had been prepared beforehand by the officials, and circulated to the other side, so the proceedings were not informative. This was followed by the other side presenting its case (this was also well known in advance). Then the discussion would be thrown open, and those wishing to make their names would speak. Then some questions would be replied to, but not answered. (Some time in the middle we would be given tea or coffee and a biscuit to the maximum disturbance of the proceedings.) Then the meeting would end with the Secretary of State/Minister saying what a very valuable meeting it had been. More chortling noises and gestures would ensue and we would be ushered out.

Nothing was *ever* decided at any of these meetings which I attended. Heaven knows what they cost the wretched taxpayer if they had been properly costed out. The clear impression to be gained from these rituals was as if two obese and partially blind prize-fighters had been brought out of retirement. In the ring each proved to be too tired to fight, advanced towards the centre and, recognising his old opponent, patted him affectionately on the shoulder before retreating rather ponderously to his own corner. I got into the most fearful trouble on one occasion for daring to be cross with the genial Edmund Dell who was then Paymaster-General and who happened to be a politician for whom I have had a great admiration ever since an occasion at a meeting of L.E.F.T.A. when he outlined with great lucidity how little a government can actually do. On this occasion he was unprepared to give us an indication of how the Government viewed the long-term trend in interest rates. It may have been true (as Illtyd averred) that I had had too good a lunch that day, but if the Treasury couldn't give us some guidance on our long-term borrowing strategy, who on earth could?

Occasionally a decision would come from Whitehall, but it would be totally unexpected, and not a political but a technical decision with far-reaching consequences on which the politicians were not consulted. Thus, because at the end of 1975 the Department of the Environment's "subsidies manual" was amended to prohibit the cost of staff engaged on capital works from being charged to housing revenue account, some £5 million of the G.L.C.'s capital expenditure had suddenly to be switched from revenue to capital account involving an additional borrowing requirement of £10 million for 1975/6 and 1976/7. The poor old London ratepayer lost a cool £3½ million of housing subsidy in 1975/6 and £3 million in 1976/7 to central government and no politician had taken a decision at all. The machine was so *big* that no one seemed to know what anyone else was doing. Those who are actually in the decision-making process in politics have a vested interest in pretending that it is less chaotic than it really is. For, if it is chaotic, why are they bothering?

The first instance I will cite of the machine actually taking over control happened at a meeting in the Leader's room on 26 February 1976 which was concerned with the basis upon which certain G.L.C. property was to be transferred to the London boroughs. The affair had a long history. The large-scale transfer of property and interests in property which accompanied the redistribution of functions under the London Government Act of 1963 created many areas where there were differences of opinion between the G.L.C. and the London boroughs about the proper basis on which land should be vested.

By 1976, these differences of opinion had mostly been resolved but there remained two areas of disagreement on which agreement could not be reached. These were (*a*) non-housing properties on transferred housing estates and (*b*) land zoned for public open space but held by the G.L.C. for other purposes. The London Boroughs Association (an extremely effective and economical institution as I have previously mentioned) had asked for another member-level meeting to discuss these two matters but the

Director-General thought we should first have a meeting to consider whether we would agree to a further meeting. The meeting on 26 February was this meeting about a meeting.

The Director-General pointed out that the matter had repeatedly and extensively been considered at policy level. The terms of transfer, although complicated to the layman, were well understood by the professional. In the case of non-housing properties on transferred housing estates, commercial properties were to be transferred at market value, all other properties at outstanding debt but with certain safeguards as to nomination rights and pre-emption rights for land with development potential. In the case of land zoned for open space, land in C.D.A. grant-unit was to be covered at nil value; slum clearance sites at original cost; and land where the G.L.C.'s holding was 75 per cent or more of zoned open space, at outstanding debt but with pre-emption rights as a safeguard against inaction by the borough council or against change to more valuable use. Other land was to be transferred at market value.

I give all this information to indicate what a lot of time had clearly been given to this problem. The suggestion for the meeting which we were holding the meeting to decide upon, had come from the Housing and Works Committee of the L.B.A. and was said to be made in "one final attempt to reach an overall agreement between the L.B.A. and the G.L.C. which the L.B.A. could then recommend boroughs to accept". The two topics had hitherto been considered quite separately and had nothing in common except that in both the L.B.A. were seeking still further concessions as to the financial terms of transfer. The Director-General was doubtful of the value of a meeting at which we should not be able to concede anything more.

When I looked at the papers (it was the first time I had been concerned in the dispute) I could not for the life of me see why we should *not* make further concessions. The situation was precisely analogous to a transfer of property between wholly-owned subsidiaries of the same parent company. The land was the undivided property of precisely the same people: the shareholders in the parent company (in our case the ratepayers of London); and it did not in the least matter at what price the land was conveyed as long as there was no extra tax to pay (or in our case, no grant from central government was lost).

This was not to argue that all transactions between public bodies could be done in this way. Transfers between British Rail and the G.L.C., or the Port of London Authority and the G.L.C. involve different principles, because the transferor and transferee are fed from a different tax (and charges) base. But in the case of the G.L.C. and the London boroughs, the tax base was precisely the same and provided the rich boroughs were not being further enriched at the expense of the poor (which I was assured they were not) it did not matter a fig at what price the vesting took place. In my view we should have stopped wasting time and conceded the boroughs everything they wanted.

When, at the Leader's behest, I put this view at the meeting to decide about a meeting, I was greeted with a howl of protest from the officers. The only substantial argument produced against my view was that morale in the valuers department, which (I was told) was already at an all-time low, would fall below the floor if the G.L.C. were to take my line. In other words, the machine had taken over, and the fight had to go on to satisfy the protagonists although no ratepayer was affected in any way by this extremely costly (in officer time) delay in getting things settled.

I would have understood it if it had only been the officers who took this line, but this was not so. The Leader had assembled some of his ablest chairmen of committees for the meeting. I was quite alone in my judgment that it was a storm in a tea-cup blown up to save the *amour propre* of the bureaucracy on both sides. The danger from the public's point of view is that it *suits* most politicians to keep the machine well-fed and growing, however futile its activities, because they think it extends their own power.

I consider my next instance to be more unhealthy because it

involves a commitment to *secrecy* which I find sinister. It concerns the award of the Central Arbitration Committee, dated 26 April 1976, to increase to £472 (from £416) the London weighting of G.L.C./I.L.E.A. A.P.T.E.C. and senior officers backdated to 1 July 1975.

This too had a history. In August 1974 it was agreed by the G.L.C./I.L.E.A. Whitley Council for A.P.T.E.C. staff that London weighting would be reviewed annually in the light of special published cost data for London (weighted for housing, travel and other costs) relating to the month of April in any year with any agreed increase to operate from the following July.

The data for April 1975 provided good ammunition for the staff side to launch a claim and they duly asked for an extra £72.70 per head per annum from 1 July 1975. The G.L.C./I.L.E.A. responded with an offer of £16 per head. The Arbitration Committee (one of the more pernicious ingredients of the System) split the difference at £56 per head per annum. I was for not paying them anything at all because it was agreed on all sides that there was no need for any payment to be made to maintain staff and service levels as they were. We were in the middle of a serious economic crisis and everyone was being asked to tighten their belts. But (as usual) our case had been seriously weakened by central government. In answer to a parliamentary question the Secretary of State had said that the £6 per week pay increase limit (under the then incomes policy) would apply to increases negotiable after 1 August, and the London weighting review was negotiable from 1 July and therefore outside the net; and central government soon afterwards agreed an increase of London weighting to the civil servants and so established a clear precedent for the G.L.C./I.L.E.A. staff.

But the fact that central government had behaved irresponsibly was no reason for us to follow suit. I raised the matter with the Leader (who was personally very sympathetic to my point of view) and he raised it with the Director-General; and got back the answer that "... any attempt to avoid payment would undoubtedly damage severely our relationship in our joint negotiating machinery. We could only expect the staff sides to take us to court—successfully—if we declined to pay".

So, that was that. We were stuck. I agreed that we could not refuse to pay the award but wrote to the Leader on 13 May: "What worries me is that the *machinery* for settling disputes etc. seems to have taken over control from the *parties* thereto. No reasonable man can defend paying the increase (which, as you are aware, costs every Londoner the equivalent of a ½p rate) at this juncture in our economic crisis. Reason seems to have no place in the decision which finally emerges. I am aware that it is ½p *gross* but it is symptomatic of the unreason in our affairs that most of any allowance we get for it in the R.S.G. is distributed to authorities outside London. What on earth we are to do about this state of affairs I cannot imagine, but ought we not to consider giving the fact of our impotence an airing?" I also put down a motion at the next Group meeting: "THAT the Group: (i) is appalled [at the award]; (ii) notes that this award will cost the London ratepayer the equivalent of an extra ½p rate and considers this to be an unjustifiable and unnecessary burden on Londoners; (iii) endorses the action of the Leadership in paying the award to the G.L.C. staff because there is no alternative; but (iv) feels that the fact of the G.L.C.'s impotence on this very important matter should be aired in public by a motion to Council or other appropriate step."

The reason I think that this instance of the machine taking over is more sinister than my previous instance, is that this time my fellow politicians would not let the matter be exposed to the public. My trouble (they said gently but firmly) was that I knew nothing whatever about industrial relations (which was true) and it would be disastrous for an employer to question the intricate machinery which had been built up over the years to settle industrial disputes. But what, I replied, if this intricate machinery was about to push us over the precipice? Anyway, the Leader's Co-ordinating Group (the Leader's cabinet) voted to require me to withdraw my motion from the Group meeting, which I duly did. I then took the dubious step of alerting Leslie Freeman (the opposition leader on the Establishments Board) and Horace Cutler (the opposition leader on the Policy and Resources Committee) to what was happening, but found that I could not get either of them to take the matter sufficiently seriously to raise a fuss about it. They felt that there was nothing to be gained out of trying to upset or question an arbitration award.

Finally, before the matter went to Council on 21 July, I wrote in desperation to Joe Rogaly of the *Financial Times* in the hope of interesting him enough to make the matter public. But he, although sympathetic, was bunged up with other topics. He suggested another journalist by name: but I did not want to have a sensation made out of the issue (it wasn't sensational, it was happening all the time), I wanted the thinking public to appreciate where we were all heading. So this critical fact that the machinery for arbitrating awards was leading us willy-nilly to disastrous increases in annual expenditure was never even aired. That wise man Stanley Mayne, the chairman of the Establishments Board, accused me of being obsessed with this issue. I don't think I would want to defend myself against this charge. The bureaucrats have succeeded in insulating themselves against the economic climate *at the expense* of the rest of the country at precisely the time the rest can least afford to pay.

At the end of September 1975, Illtyd Harrington (my chairman) became ill and was away from County Hall until the beginning of January 1976. Thus for three months (during the preparation of the 1976 Budget) I was acting chairman of the Policy and Resources Committee. I set out part of a (self-explanatory) aide-memoire I sent to the Leader on 2 October 1975 because it provides the background to my third and final example of the machine having taken over. "I thought it might be useful", I wrote, "if I set out my remembrance of what we discussed at our meeting on 30 September, the first occasion on which I spoke to you as acting chairman of the Policy and Resources Committee. I am having this typed at home and I do not expect you to confirm (or otherwise) my account of the conversation. It makes no mention of the immediate business in hand: the meeting of P. & R. on 1 October 1975. I told you that ever since I became connected with P. & R. I had been exercising my mind about the G.L.C.'s appalling administrative performance and how this could be improved. This was not a matter about which we could throw the blame on anyone else. Our record was giving public sector management a very bad name and we must do something about it. After quite a time discussing the problem with colleagues and G.L.C. officers, I have come to the firm conclusion that major surgery is needed . . ."

I went on to list the people I thought should go and ended up by saying that when this had been done, we should tackle the one department whose total inadequacy was a constant source of embarrassment to us. During my three months as acting chairman I was never able to get anything done on these lines, but I put this down to the Leader's justifiable reluctance to do anything while Harrington was away. This is perhaps the place for me to put on record my admiration for Sir Reg Goodwin, his patience, knowledge of local government, long-suffering wisdom and sheer skill as a politician in handling his Group and the Council. I hope that nothing I have written in this book will be taken as a criticism of him personally. He was doing all he could in the cause of sanity. I am honoured to have been allowed to serve under him.

But as the result of a further incident, I came to the conclusion that it seemed to be impossible for even the most resolute political leader to sack a chief officer at all. In the summer of 1976, we became aware that the incompetence of the department I had mentioned to the Leader in my *aide-mémoire*, was going to cost the G.L.C. over the succeeding years money in excess of £30 million. The affair was a disaster and the department needed to be totally reorganised so that this sort of thing did not happen again.

When a player's shorts get dramatically torn in a game of rugby football, it is the custom of the other players to form a scrum round him so that he can change into a new pair hidden from the view of any curious spectators. When it was suggested that the chief officer of this offending department should be asked to resign in the light of what his department had cost the Council, the action of the other chief officers could best be described as analogous to that of other rugby players when one of them loses his pants. I would like to stress that I am not accusing the chief officers of the G.L.C. of doing anything improper. Loyalty to one's colleagues and subordinates is perhaps the most important attribute of the successful administrator.

But there is a very important difference between the public and the private sector in this respect. In the private sector, there is a powerful motive for getting rid of an incompetent colleague which does not obtain in the public sector. In the private sector you may have to sack your best friend in order to preserve your own skin. In the public sector incompetence in high places can only be operated on by the politicians, and if the politicians cannot sack their civil servants, then nobody can. Incompetence feeds on itself and the cancer grows.

It was when the full implications of this last example of the machine taking over began to sink into my understanding that I began to wonder what on earth I was doing at the G.L.C. I found the life extremely enjoyable and if I had been amusing myself quite harmlessly there was no reason not to carry on. But I was amusing myself at huge expense to the ratepayer (and taxpayer). The gigantic charade in which it is true I had only a small part was costing my fellow citizens a needless fortune. I was a villain for being associated with it. I had spent the first fifty years of my life, very unsuccessfully it is true, trying as it were to get astride a vacuum. I must get out at once and try to make amends.

I had originally expected that the publication of the Houghton Report would provide me with an excuse to leave the Labour Party and the G.L.C. in a way which would cause Sir Reg and my other colleagues and friends on the G.L.C. the minimum of embarrassment. But when that report was at last published in August 1976, the Labour Government ducked the issue of whether or not to accept the majority recommendations. As

Stanley Mayne had predicted, the majority proposed that the party political machines be subsidised by the taxpayer. If that happened the System would become all powerful, but I could not afford to wait for the Government to make up its mind. The London Labour Party was heaving itself into action for the 1977 G.L.C. elections and there was to be a special party conference on election policy on 18 September 1976, at which I was to present the paper on finance.

Little bits of evidence continued to pour in that the central government of Great Britain was suffering from a terminal cancer. We were in a serious economic crisis and local authorities were under extreme pressure to reduce expenditure (but without adding to the pool of unemployed), but on 23 August, the Secretary of State for Scotland announced that Margaret Herbison, aged sixty-nine, had been appointed at a salary of £2,400 per annum for a two-day week as "public watchdog" to investigate allegations about treatment by the Law Society of public complaints against Scottish solicitors or their employees.

On 31 August *The Times* carried a huge Government advertisement for more lawyers—"as a lawyer in Government service, you could be influencing decisions affecting the whole nation's progress: economic, social, industrial, commercial or environmental". It was their remuneration which dazzled me: "Joining the Legal Service in London at age 23 your starting salary would be £4,485; at 32 or over it would be £5,800. There are promotion prospects to Senior Legal Assistant (£7,400–£9,215) within 3–6 years and to higher posts carrying salaries up to £18,675. Very able candidates aged 27 or over could enter at the Senior level immediately." So keen were central government to get applicants that a twenty-four-hour answering service was available to give further details and send application forms.

On 2 September 1976 I resigned from the Council, and at 2 p.m. on 3 September I issued a statement to the Press Association which had been agreed with the Leader's office and was to come out after it had been officially announced that I had resigned as an alderman. "I have resigned from my Constituency

Labour Party," it went. "There is no question of my seeking to join the Conservative Party. Had I felt inclined to do so, I would have remained an alderman of the G.L.C. On 27 August I wrote to the Leader: 'In the last few months I have undergone a thorough political conversion. I have become wholly convinced of the thesis, which has been argued for some time by James Robertson and Peter Cadogan, that the most important single cause of this country's ills is over-mighty government (of which the G.L.C. is, alas, a significant example). I have been impressed by our near total powerlessness as politicians to do anything about it. I have come to the conclusion that the best solution is to try to dismantle this ruinously costly edifice we have all built up before it is too late. In these circumstances it would be quite wrong of me, in the period leading up to next year's G.L.C. election, to take part in a campaign in which I do not believe' . . ."

I need not have bothered. By now I was a totally unimportant person. No newspaper thought my statement worth mentioning.

CHAPTER TEN

THE FUTURE

WHAT then must we do?

What is needed more than anything else is a change of heart, attitude or principle—whichever of these three connected concepts spur people to action. The men who seek to get to the top of government in order to have power over their fellows must be recognised for what they are: evil men engaged upon an immoral purpose. Good government is no longer about power, but about the mechanics of reconciling people's interests and just ambitions. As James Robertson has said (Op. cit., p. 74): "The idea that clever people, climbing to strategic peaks in the structure of society and thence surveying social and economic questions from a great height, can make objective assessments of costs and benefits, right and wrong, true and false, that will be valid for us all—that is one of the biggest lies in the soul of institutional man."

What we have to do, as carefully and considerately as we can, is to *dismantle* the existing structure of government and *decentralise* decision-taking as far and as fast as it can be done.

In the days when central government's chief job was to run an army and navy, conduct foreign affairs and rule an empire, it was appropriate that, in Great Britain, its functions should be centralised. But the task of government is now quite different. The country's expenditure on education alone exceeds the defence budget (although the latter is far more burdensome to the balance of payments because much of it passes across the exchanges into other currencies). Nobody knows what the best way of educating the young is. There are no economies of scale or other arguments which can be validly made for requiring children all over England and Wales to conform to the same pattern. What is emphatically *not* needed is a central policy. What is needed is the maximum variety of different schools and institutions of learning. Similarly with health, housing and the personal social services. We all want *more* resources spent on them (which we shall *not* get) but nobody knows what the right balance between public and private spending on health (or education for that matter) should be; or how best to cope with an ageing population. What right have some people to seek to force their *mores* on all their fellow citizens?

All we *know* about our current national housing problem is that it does not work. I have my own pet solution to this problem in the case of London which I have already expounded in these pages. But the problems of Leeds or Merioneth may be totally different, and not amenable to my suggested remedies. It is of the first importance that there should be as much diversity and experiment in these *increasingly important* areas of good government as possible. It may well be that what is successful in one region, may not succeed in another. We are not all alike, thank God. As a nation, we ought not to *want* decisions on education, housing, health and the personal social services to be taken centrally. We need a massive devolution of power over them, from Westminster to the people who use them. In practical terms this means a devolution of the power to tax.

There is in practice, if not in theory, no devolution of political power in Britain today. Because of its nearly complete control of their sources of cash, the central government has the local authorities precisely where it wants them—as puppets on a string. One of the more disagreeable revelations to come out of Crossman's *Diaries* is the relish with which he upset local planning decisions (although he was candid enough to admit that he made mistakes) for no better reason than that he was cock of the roost and had the ultimate power.

This was not always so. In the old days when the Chamberlains were making their mark on Birmingham, and more recently when Herbert Morrison was making his mark on the old L.C.C., the local authorities possessed quite a considerable amount of autonomy. What has happened to alter the balance of power? The explanation is the source of the money. Before 1880, local government was self-supporting. In 1890 roughly 75 per cent of all local authority income came from sources they controlled themselves—the rates and miscellaneous non-trading income. Today, only £1 in every £3 raised in taxation to finance local government expenditure is raised through the rates. What is even more important is that growth in local government expenditure has depended upon a growth in the proportion of expenditure financed by national taxation. The trend has been clear for the last eighty-five years.

But, it will be argued, what does this matter if central government makes up to the required level, through some fair mechanism, the money which is needed to perform the duties which are, in theory, delegated to the local authorities? The Rate Support Grant, it will be argued, gives the local authorities all the resources they can reasonably need within the constraints demanded by the national economy. But as I have already shown, the Rate Support Grant is a shambles—an absurdity. It is the *reductio ad absurdum* of the whole system of government: *reductio ad absurdum*, in this context, being a valid method of inferring the undesirability of a policy by showing that its consequences lead to an absurdity.

Since the end of the 1939–45 war there have been three attempts, of different kinds, to reorganise local government in England. There was first the Trustram Eve Commission of 1947; then the Hancock Commission of 1961–4 and the Redcliffe-Maud Royal Commission leading to the Local Government Act of 1972. All have set about their tasks from the wrong end. They have looked at local government; they have examined the powers and responsibilities of the various authorities; they have suggested institutions which should exercise the delegated powers and responsibilities; they have examined how the elected representatives of the various authorities should be chosen and they have *assumed* that the money would be found somewhere. It is wholly typical that the Layfield Enquiry should have been set up *after* Peter Walker's mammoth local government reorganisation. It is again typical that the current great debate on devolution to Scotland and Wales should have commenced on the basis that central government will continue to hold the purse strings; and I rejoice that the Scottish Nationalists are not standing for that arrogance.

This is to go about the problem precisely the wrong way round. What *matters* is the power to raise money, as the long struggle for supremacy between the Monarch and Parliament, and then between the House of Lords and the House of Commons, has clearly shown. The powers that are to be devolved, the regions into which the country is to be divided, and the institutions which are to be given the responsibilities—these are very much subsidiary questions. What I am saying is not new—it has been common ground in local government circles for years, and has been in print since 1972, when M. F. Stonefrost (the distinguished and extremely capable Comptroller of Financial Services at the G.L.C.) published his address to the annual local government conference of the Conservative Party. The only important question in the whole devolution debate is what taxes (or other sources of revenue) is central government prepared to allow out of its grip? Unless Westminster is prepared to cede some of its revenue-raising powers to the regions, we may as well abandon the great debate at once.

I do not minimise the nature of this task. To get something done will be an almighty battle, against a very powerful army of entrenched interests—not least the whole of Whitehall. The House of Commons, that great bastion of democracy, has never devolved any of its powers to tax. The rates are left over from the days of monarchical government and are now totally inadequate for the tasks central government has heaped on the local authorities, and for the maintenance of responsible local government—which is why we are saddled with the R.S.G. In theory the customs and excise duties could be devolved, but in practice we can all see that it would be impractical to move in that direction within the European Common Market (which is devoted to abolishing customs duties between its members);

corporation tax could not be fairly devolved (although I would argue that the Scots could have it if they want it) without making worse the trouble which central governments are already experiencing with the multi-national corporations and their propensity to channel profits into tax havens; the V.A.T. could be a candidate but it is the chosen tax base of the E.E.C. This leaves us with income tax; and in choosing income tax I have the support of the majority of the Layfield Committee.

The amount raised in income tax by central government in 1975–6 was estimated at around £14,000 million. As it happens, this is broadly equal to the total expenditure on the main personal services undertaken by government (education, health, social services, etc.) whether they are carried out by local authorities or by the undemocratic "QUANGO's", like the area health authorities, the proliferation of which in recent years has been such a significant symptom of Westminster's determination to divide and rule. Not only are these personal services now the most important function of government, but their importance will grow as functions like foreign affairs and defence move inexorably to Brussels. As I have argued, it is most important for the recipients of these services that they shall *not* be run centrally. So I go further than Layfield and propose that the whole proceeds of the income tax should be ceded by Westminster to local government and the Treasury should exercise its control over the economy (if at all) through its other taxes.

Having decided to devolve the income tax, the next question is: to which tier of local government should the power to raise the income tax be delegated? My unequivocal answer, on the principle that you must try to get power down the line as far from the centre as you can, is the *bottom* tier of government—to the boroughs in London and the equivalent institutions in the conurbations, and to the districts in the counties. Of course, some of the services to be paid for by the income tax will be better provided for by larger units, but there is no reason why the lower authorities should not voluntarily combine together for the purpose of providing them. After some experience of its inner workings, I can give it as my considered opinion that there is nothing which the G.L.C. now does which could not as effectively and democratically (and more economically) be done by appropriate committees of the L.B.A., were the L.B.A. to be given the necessary powers by Westminster. I detect in the I.L.E.A. (after the Auld Committee on the William Tyndale Schools) a movement towards giving more powers to the individual boroughs—and if that trend continues there is no reason why an association of the inner London boroughs should not run any common services required by the schools and other learning institutions in the I.L.E.A. area, and make that tier of government otiose.

Before thinking people reject out of hand a proposal to give more power to the town hall and the local politicians, on the grounds that they are even worse than their counterparts at Westminster, let them reflect that this may be a direct consequence of the present centralised System. If Westminster is the only place where genuine decisions can be taken, it will attract all the able people, like bees round the honey-pot. If all the decisions are taken at Westminster, there is no point in anyone who wants to get anything done wasting his time at the town hall (or at County Hall). When my colleagues and I looked wistfully from County Hall across the river to the Houses of Parliament, there was not a single one of us who could (honestly) say that we would not rather have been on the other side of the river. Efforts to strengthen and improve local democracy have been doomed to failure from the outset by the way in which the System has taken steps to see that decision-taking is centralised.

Since education and health would form such a large proportion of the services a local authority would provide, the local income tax should be assessed on the basis of residence, not place of work. The Inland Revenue has conceded to the Layfield Enquiry that this would be possible (although expensive). The expense would be greatly reduced if income tax could be simplified. So simplification of the administration of the income tax must, at once, be a primary objective of national policy even if it involves a degree of inequity between taxpayers. Income tax is now incomprehensible, and causing an administrative log-jam of which we have not yet heard the full effect. Of course there would be need of a device for equalising the proceeds of the income tax, so that rich authorities aided the poorer authorities, but the L.B.A. already manages a rate equalisation scheme without any powers of compulsion—and there is no reason at all why an income tax equalisation scheme should not be equally effective, worked out between themselves by the bottom-tier authorities and not imposed on them by Westminster. As the new system of government grows in strength, it is not absurdly idealistic to hope that legislation about industrial relations and "unemployment" benefits could be transferred from Westminster to the local authorities. I say this because it is another area in which there needs to be a total change of heart.

As a result of deliberate and intelligent human endeavour (as I wrote in the spring 1976 *L.E.F.T.A. Quarterly*), there is, at long last, nothing like enough paid work to be done in the British Isles. (In this respect we are, once again, pioneering the world.) Much of everyone's most satisfying endeavour is devoted to the business of saving work. At the family level this is evidenced in the achievement of better-designed houses, easier ways of keeping warm, labour-saving machines and more easily cooked food. At the business level, no piece of machinery has been installed in the last twenty-five years which has not had, as a primary objective, that labour should be saved. On the administrative level a computer can do tasks in a few minutes which would have needed many thousands of intelligent manhours before the war.

We are a small, extremely rich country, fully exploited by an industrious, honest and intelligent population of over fifty million people. Is it at all surprising, therefore, that after twenty-five years of the endeavour described in the previous paragraph:

(i) the steel industry has 144,000 workers too many;

(ii) the railways have nearer 200,000 and the Post Office more than 100,000 too many;

(iii) many hundreds of millions of pounds are needed to keep jobs going in the vehicle and aircraft industries in order to produce machines for which there is no obvious use;

(iv) car manufacturers, London docks, newspapers, ship-builders (you name it, we have them) are all so seriously over-manned as to threaten their very existence, without large subsidies of one sort or another from the taxpayer?

No, it should not be a matter of surprise. But the conventional reaction to "unemployment" needs to be radically re-examined. It should not be a matter for lamentation that there are over one and a half million unemployed. We should rejoice, because it gives us a chance to share out the unavoidable work-load more evenly. A great number of people in Britain today work far too hard. Among others, nearly all mothers with two or more children under ten years old, nurses in sole charge of chronically sick or disabled persons, not to mention vehicle-assembly workers doing overtime.

We should be bending our very considerable intelligence and powers of organisation to cope with the idiotic situation with which we shall shortly be faced in which half the population will be working with ever-diminishing returns for extra effort, in order to keep the other half in unsought idleness. The British workers (unlike the commentators) are beginning to see this. There is slummy living in Britain all right, but not among the workers. Why should they work harder to keep an idiotic System going? Of course they strike at the drop of a hat.

What is the solution? The *Economist* of 3 January 1976 had some interesting ideas: more one-day public holidays, sabbaticals, longer holidays, etc., but to my mind they would touch only the fringe of the problem. (One certain way *not* to cure the problem is part of today's conventional wisdom: that local authority spending must be drastically cut. There has been significant growth in local authority expenditure—apart from increased interest charges—in only two areas in the last ten years:

in personal social services and in education. Neither can be categorised as a waste of scarce resources.)

If I were a revolutionary. I would advocate a compulsory three/four-day week; not for businesses but for workers. People would either work the short week Friday to Sunday; or the long week Monday to Thursday; but not both. The same shops, banks, offices, factories, plant and machinery would be used and the managers could (if they liked) work both weeks. The managers can be relied upon to look after themselves in one way or another—or else they should not be managers. As a nation we managed perfectly adequately in Edward Heath's three-day week. What was lost could well have been made up, if idle plant and machinery were being worked by other hands. But I am not a revolutionary and I suppose that we must come gradually upon the horizon to which I am raising up my eyes.

Unemployment and industrial relations is another area in which, as a people, we are groping for an answer. We urgently need to hedge our bets in a way which is impossible when all decisions of any consequence are either (and most probably) not taken at all, or taken at national level.

What would there be left for Westminster to do? It is to be hoped that there would be very little. There would be the vestigial power to run the currency, foreign affairs and defence until these powers were eventually transferred to the ambit of the E.E.C.'s decision-making machinery. The regions of England and Wales (but not Scotland) would perhaps wish that the criminal law be legislated about centrally, but otherwise, it is to be hoped that variety would have full sway. The House of Commons can then be reformed so that it contained the same number of members, was elected on the same boundaries and by the same electoral system, as Great Britain's representatives in the European Parliament. It would then meet to discuss how its members were to conduct themselves in the large assembly.

And the House of Lords? There may be a case for a permanent assembly of peers (drawn from all the estates in the realm) to scrutinise the by-laws passed by the local authorities; and a permanent judicial committee to interpret a Bill of Rights. There may also be a case for opening up its membership so that we should have peers of the realm from our Common Market partners. It might then, eventually, come to occupy the position of the whole E.E.C.'s second chamber. Perhaps our Monarch may become Empress (or Emperor) of Europe.

But enough of this sort of cloud-cuckoo land. The immediate practical moves are to simplify the income tax so that the power to levy a residence based tax can be devolved to the lowest of the present tiers of government. These will then be powered with the resources, and saddled with the responsibility, of providing the public sector end of all the personal social services, including health and education. It is a perfectly manageable programme and would suit the Scottish and Welsh Nationalists.

In explaining how he came to call his book *A Spiritual Aeneid* (Longmans, 1918), Ronald Knox wrote: "Not very long ago the Archbishop of Canterbury, animadverting upon the varied religious experiences of a certain free-lance Bishop, described them as 'an episcopal Odyssey'. The phrase is wanting in aptness, when it is remembered that, wherever your Odyssey takes you, it must involve coming back home at the end of it. I have dared to take my title from a poem even richer in associations. For an Aeneid involves not merely coming home, but coming home to a place you have never been in before—one that combines in itself all that you valued in the old home with added promises of a future that is new."

In my political Aeneid, I certainly have not returned to the Conservative faith of my youth. It is not called the Conservative and Unionist Party for nothing; and I can see no merit in aspiring once more to a Great Britain. What I have been searching for is a dream of getting a rational order into our affairs that has been missing for a great number of years. I now attribute this disorder to size. *Small may not be beautiful but obesity is always ugly*. The important lesson to be learned from our present failure is that, in a democracy, if the system gets too big, complicated and *fat*, you cease to get sensible decisions out of the machinery for making them.

May I illustrate this with a homely example that I have come to consider to be more and more significant? I survived, only on the chairman's casting vote, a vote of no confidence put at a meeting of the Ealing Acton Constituency Labour Party on the question of raising London's bus and underground fares in 1974. My argument—that either fares had to go up or the rates had to go up because central government was prepared to pay no more—was met by the argument that fares should not go up and rates should not go up and that central government should be *made* to pay more. No amount of corroboration from the leader of the Ealing Council (and president of the C.L.P.) and others that not only would central government pay no more, but was threatening to reduce the Transport Supplementary Grant unless we raised fares, had any persuasive power.

My opponents were *not* left-wing extremists. By no yardstick were they unintelligent. The truth is that the System is now so complicated as to be incomprehensible, not just to the man in the street, but to me also—despite my having devoted a considerable part of my life (as this book has sought to testify) to trying to find out. How can you expect local authorities to be economical when for every £1 of ratepayers' money they spend, Santa Claus gives them a bonus of £2? How can you expect wage restraint when the Government offers a newly qualified lawyer (trained at the taxpayers' expense) £4,485 per annum at age twenty-three with a career structure that may eventually bring him in £18,675 per annum with an index-linked pension geared to his final earnings? How can you expect industrial democracy to flourish when terms of service hammered out on the shop-floor are subject to the next prices and incomes policy? or businesses to invest in new machinery when tomorrow they may be subjected to a prices and dividend freeze? How do you reconcile people to the need for austerity when the Government appoints a sixty-nine-year-old ex-colleague to do a job which almost certainly doesn't need doing, at a salary of £2,400 per annum for a two-day week? The list of unanswerable questions is inexhaustible. Politics is not so much a *dirty* business as totally incomprehensible.

If you want to get sensible decisions by democratic means, then the System must be simple, so that ordinary voters can understand it. If the System is not simple, you will not get sensible decisions. It is as simple as that. I am sufficiently committed to democracy to believe that we can still get sensible decisions from our present System if we move to decentralise decision-taking in the way I have outlined.

EPILOGUE

I AM going to end by making some wild guesses at the kind of simplification of government which could be achieved within a very few years and at great savings in time, money and frustration, if the various changes of heart I have outlined took place.

I will begin with tax, because it is an area of government I have always been particularly interested in, and in which we are wholly masters of our own destiny and cannot blame anyone else if things go wrong. It is an area in which we are doing deplorably badly at the moment. I would like to preface these guesses with an uncharacteristic note of hesitation. The matters I am writing about are so technical that I doubt if any single person knows all parts of the machine well enough to be sure how any particular measure will affect the individuals it is designed to reach. But (as I said earlier) something must be done as a matter of urgency to simplify the tax structure. With the *Financial Times* calling for the taxation of supplementary benefits, the patently absurd situation is nearly upon us when one end of our government bureaucracy is building up to take away the money which another growing bureaucracy is trying to distribute.

My first guess is that every individual person over the age of eighteen, whether male or female, married or single, employed, unemployed, pensioned or leisured, could have paid into his/her bank, national giro, or national savings bank account, a certain *basic weekly credit* (or negative income tax, if you prefer that term) of, say, £10 (at October 1976 prices) in exchange for all the personal allowances (where claimable) now built into our income tax system. Any pension or benefit they might then be receiving from the state would simultaneously be reduced by £10 per week. For children under the age of eighteen, their mothers could be credited with £5 in place of the various child benefit schemes which now obtain.

All other income (i.e. other than the weekly credit) could be taxed at a flat rate of, say, 50 per cent at source by whoever paid the income, and the payer would account therefor to government. Thus, all employees, irrespective of their present marriage allowances, child allowances, child benefits, national insurance contributions, life insurance reductions, mortgage interest reliefs, etc. now earning £100 per week (£5,200 per annum) would get £10 from government, £45 from their employer and their employer would double up what he paid the employee (£45) and pay this (plus £10) over to government. For those earning £50 per week, the figure for each employee would be: £10 from government, £20 from their employer and their employer would deduct £20 tax and pay this (plus £10) to government. The same would happen *mutatis mutandis* with salaried staff, but the benefit from government would be paid to everyone on a weekly basis. The spouses of those who were married and not in paid employment would also get the basic weekly credit.

It is to be noted that this would not prevent a local authority from varying the rate of a local income tax. Thus, if a local authority's rate were less than 50 per cent it could account to its resident taxpayer for the excess deducted at source; and, if more, it could raise an additional assessment.

The rent of one unit of accommodation per individual could be paid by that individual *net* of tax at 50 per cent (and if that individual did not earn any taxable income, this would be a bonus to him or her) so that if her rent was £20 per week, she would pay her landlord (whether private or public sector) £10 per week. This measure could be conveniently combined with a relaxation of rent controls to enable private sector rents to double.

Mortgage interest on any loan secured on one unit of accommodation per individual could be paid net of tax. Building societies would pay interest after deducting tax at 50 per cent, and their expenses would come out of any "turn" provided between net income and net expenditure.

Next we come to the jungle of supplementary benefits, senior citizen's pensions, unemployment pay, widow's pensions and the like. To begin with, the *basic weekly credit* would have to be supplemented in the case of these beneficiaries, but this could much best be done by leaving the method and rate at which the supplement was given to the discretion of the local authority. The *cost* of living varies considerably over the country. It is not rational to prescribe the "right" supplements for the country as a whole. It is much to be hoped that there would be variety.

It is also to be hoped that it would soon be possible to increase the basic weekly credit of £10. Then the various supplementary credits could be allowed to decrease until everyone received a basic minimum on which he or she could live whether they chose to work, study or do nothing. At this point it would be up to local communities to determine whether *anyone* should receive supplementary benefits. (It would be a corollary that anyone living in public institutions would have to contribute something towards their keep out of the basic weekly credit they received.)

The aim should be to give every individual person the right to a sufficient *dole* to enable him or her to live without working, should he or she wish to do so, *with no stigma attached.*

Next, the field of pensions: whether provided by the state or by private sector. I do not think it is sufficiently appreciated what a distorting influence the tremendous business of providing pensions has upon our economy and lives. First, it makes it very much more difficult to maintain any mobility of employment after age forty (even with compulsory transferable pension rights). Secondly, it ensures that some services are made very much more expensive than they need be because of the necessity of huge funding payments. (It has also to be mentioned that there was scarcely a pension fund in the country which was not technically insolvent during the 1974 Stock Exchange "low".) Thirdly, it has already spawned a colossal bureaucracy of actuaries, accountants, inland revenue officials, tax advisers, investment experts of very high calibre (because there is a lot of money in this business) to no productive end whatever. Fourthly, it provides many pensioners with a miserable old age because, although they have enough money, they do not feel wanted. This list of distortions is by no means exhaustive.

Therefore, at some stage in the simplification process, not only could the whole process of employees' national insurance contributions, but also employers' contributions, be scrapped. No employer would be allowed to deduct his contributions towards any private pension arrangement from his gross profits for tax purposes. Then private pension funds can be wound up and the proceeds distributed forthwith among the persons entitled to them: the past and present subscribers. Public sector pensions (if any) would no longer be funded even if there is a case for funding them now, and the whole business of providing pensions could (for the future) be eliminated. There is, of course, no reason why individuals should not purchase annuities for themselves out of their savings, but the present system by which people's whole lives are geared to their pensions at a certain age, and their worth is measurable by their pension rights, must come to an end.

The aim should be to allow people to retire whenever they like (and come back to work again if they wish). Employers can then get rid of employees with the minimum of hardship at any age.

In the field of education, instead of government paying anything towards someone's education after age eighteen, my guess is that it would be cheaper to pay at birth a bounty of, say, £500 into a national giro account for every child born in this country, which would earn interest, but which he or she would not be allowed to cash until his or her eighteenth birthday. It would then be theirs to do with what they liked—either to spend on higher education or to devote to some less high-minded cause.

Finally, in the field of industrial relations, there can be no justification for the present practice of making public sector employees virtually unsackable. My guess is that, in the end, the right way to tackle this problem (and to eliminate the outrage of extravagant service agreements leading to huge golden-handshakes) is to arrange that *all* contracts of service for more than one year (whether public or private sector) should be unenforceable at law.

As Peter Cadogan and James Robertson have rightly been insisting for some time, we are at a turning-point in the affairs of our country. Either we can go on, as we have been going on since 1945, making the System more and more complicated and costly until finally, like the gallant, gallant ship that goes three times round, we sink to the bottom of the sea in confusion. Or we can take deliberate steps to simplify the System and economise.

The guesses I have here hazarded are not meant to be more than sighting shots in the direction we should go if we are not to sink. I throw them out in the hope that others favour the same journey and are prepared to call a halt to our present idiotic and undignified gyrations.